Chasing Rainbows

Chasing Rainbows

a journey from broken promises
to the everlasting covenant

Written by RACHEL LEIGH
Artwork by JOY BARGER

Contributions made by
ANGEL KING, MCLC

XULON PRESS

Xulon Press
555 Winderley Pl, Suite 225
Maitland, FL 32751
407.339.4217
www.xulonpress.com

Contributions by Joy Barger and Angel King

Paperback ISBN-13: 978-1-66288-504-4
Ebook ISBN-13: 978-1-66288-505-1

Acknowledgements

Special thanks to Angel King for walking with me through this difficult season, encouraging me and reminding me of my identity in Christ. The advice you have given me will continue to have long-lasting impacts both practically and spiritually. Your knowledge and contributions to Chasing Rainbows are invaluable.

Many thanks to my incredibly talented sister, Joy Barger, for using her artistic gift to create the beautiful piece of art featured on the cover. Thank you for taking my vision and running with it.

Also, thanks to Michele Atkins for using your God-given skill behind the camera lens to create a timeless portrait.

I must also thank my mom and brother. Without your love and support, I'm not sure I would have seen this book all the way through. Kevin, thank you for being present from the beginning of this dark season. You used your teaching gift well, gently reminding me of the Lord's heart for me in the midst of my broken situation and encouraging me to think and act in a Gospel-based way. Thank you for helping me see the bigger picture of what the Lord was doing in my own heart.

Dr. Russ Rainey, you were the first steady and impartial voice I heard at the start of my separation. You grounded me in Christ in ways I'll never be the same for, while getting me started on the path toward healing and acceptance.

Lastly, thank you to my friends and family, including my precious small group ladies, that came alongside me and my children to support us in various ways. All four of us are better for having your love and encouragement.

Preface

And they overcame him because of the blood of the Lamb and because of the word of their testimony, and they did not love their life even when faced with death. Revelation 12:11 (NASB)

Jesus commands us to testify to the goodness of the Father (John 15:27). This is how we overcome the Evil One, by sharing our testimony. The blood of the Lamb is all over my journey. I've seen His faithful hand covering me in every step of this painful season; His hand at work is the common thread found throughout my story even from the very beginning. It's easy to miss God if you're not looking for Him. He's a gentleman, after all. The heart behind all of this is the same sentiment Paul wrote to the church at Ephesus. *I pray that the eyes of your heart may be enlightened in order that you may know the hope to which he has called you, the riches of his glorious inheritance in his holy people* (Eph. 1:18 NIV).

I'm honored you're on this journey with me to see the light in a very, very dark season. Be encouraged because the dark doesn't last forever. The Father cares deeply. *The Lord is close to the brokenhearted and saves those who are crushed in spirit* (Ps. 34:18 NIV).

"The deepest things that I have learned in my own life have come from the deepest suffering. And out of the deepest waters and the hottest fires have come the deepest things that I know about God."–Elisabeth Elliot[1]

Table of Contents

INTRODUCTION
Soul Crushing Pain

The pain of realizing my fourteen-year marriage just came to a screeching halt was excruciating. Soul crushing. Deafening. Unbearable. I truly thought I would die from the pain of the heartbreak, and if the pain wouldn't kill me, I wanted to do anything to make it stop. Yet, try as I might, nothing would stop the tears from coming. Nothing stopped my mind from spinning, constantly questioning what I did wrong and how on earth I could have possibly missed any warning signs. I hated myself for always seeing and believing the best in others. Sleep was no longer peaceful. My questioning somehow invaded my dreams. Everything I saw or heard reminded me of him, like a special memory with him or an inside joke just between the two of us. I was reminded of the history we shared at every turn. Food had no appeal whatsoever. Wine didn't taste the same anymore. It was just a means to an end. Even knowing I still had three little faces to care for, I was just so wrapped up in the heaviest grief I've ever known and couldn't possibly care for them. A tiny hug from their sweet, very concerned selves would set me back off. I could barely look them directly in the eye, knowing how their world was about to turn upside down. My prayers were angry and full of lament. I wondered where my Savior was.

This is where I was for about eight days until I met my counselor, Russ. He said, "I know it feels like you're freefalling, but because you have Jesus, He won't let you fall all the way down. He's already caught you and will carry you through this valley of the shadow of death." Death. Yes, that is exactly what it was. The death of our marriage that I treasured so much. The death of my closest friendship. Here's the thing about the valley of the shadow of death, you don't know if it's just a shadow or if it's actually going to kill you. It is a dark and lonely valley unless you have someone who walks you through it. But Jesus! His light would eventually light our way through and out of this valley.

Imagine a black backdrop, so dark because of your grief and heavy heartbreak. Then a tiny pinprick through the black happens and you see the tiniest sliver of light. That light is hope. Hope that is found only in Jesus. Those were what Russ's words did to my heart that day. It was as if Jesus Himself gave me the pinprick of light and hope. He was in control this whole time, even when nothing made sense to me. He knew this season was coming for me and would faithfully catch me, along with my tears, and carry me through. He would give me the words to say to my children to let them know their dad was not coming home. He would give me the strength to be there for my children when I didn't think I could stand or care for myself. He would eventually tear that tiny pinprick of light wide open and shed His light on all of it. His grace and mercy would cover me and my children in the coming days and months. He would make the words of Isaiah come to life for me.

> *But now, this is what the Lord says— he who created you, Jacob, he who formed you, Israel: "Do not fear, for I have redeemed you; I have summoned you by name; you are mine. When you pass through the waters, I will be with you; and when you pass through the rivers,*

they will not sweep over you. When you walk through the fire, you will not be burned; the flames will not set you ablaze. For I am the Lord your God, the Holy One of Israel, your Savior..." Isaiah 43:1-3 (NIV)

Since you picked up this book, I can imagine you can somehow relate to my story, my heartbreak. Maybe you are walking through this yourself. Perhaps you've been here before and know this kind of heartbreak intimately. Maybe you have fallen all the way down and don't know who this Jesus is I'm talking about. Wherever you are, my hope is that this serves as an encouragement to you. You won't feel so alone after reading this. You will begin to understand that the Lord orchestrates our life stories for His glory and our good, the good of those who love Him. I encourage you to seek Him and open your heart to see how this heartbreak just might be used to further His kingdom. Allow yourself to be held and wrapped up in His loving arms. Allow Him to catch your tears. You don't have to feel ashamed to be real and raw when coming into His presence. He is a Man of Sorrows and is *well* acquainted with our grief, even this heartbreak. Let that comfort you now knowing He's already felt what you feel.

Thank you for joining me on this journey. I would love to walk you through some of what I've learned through this, mostly being how the Lord has revealed Himself to me in this season. I've learned so much on the subjects of forgiveness, hope, and waiting. I've had the privilege of sharing and teaching these lessons to my kids. It wasn't just my heart that needed to learn these truths, but those three tiny faces, as well.

I heard this verse so many times along my journey. *Weeping may last through the night, but joy comes with the morning* (Ps. 30:5 NLT). While it held hope, it felt unattainable. There were days it felt like the weeping would literally never stop, but it has. And now, on the other side of this mess, I'm experiencing joy in the morning.

While never in a million years did I see myself getting a divorce or being a single mom, I can honestly say now it's probably the best thing that ever happened to me. I know that's a bold statement! You'll see why, though. God is a good, good Father.

CHAPTER 1
Broken Promises

I guess we should talk a little bit about how we got here.

I grew up in church, and I mean that pretty literally. My dad served as a music minister, so I was in the building often. I don't have a dramatic come-to-Jesus moment. I just knew one Sunday when I was six as we pulled into the church parking lot that I wanted to be able to tell my Sunday school teacher I had accepted Jesus into my heart. Knowing I was a sinner, I prayed and wanted Him to come into my life to change me. I probably said that same prayer twenty times over the course of my childhood, but that's where it all began. I know that accepting Him so young spared me from so much. For that, I'm so thankful my salvation story isn't too intense.

Fast forward a few years to when I was fourteen years old. My dad abruptly left our family. He stepped down from ministry and ran off with another without looking back very often. Before moving out, he told my two younger siblings and I that everything he taught us about our faith was a lie. It was soul crushing. We felt abandoned and utterly confused.

How could he? Why?! My dad ripped the rug right out from under all of us. I always thought he abandoned my siblings and I, but now I understand he abandoned my mom, too.

Broken hearts were everywhere. We were crushed, but I was so thankful we still had each other... until my parents decided it was best that I go live with my dad and his new partner. Then I felt like I lost my mom and siblings, too. It felt very "every man for himself." I made a couple of terrible choices in who I kept company with, but eventually, I put my head down, worked hard, and focused on school and going to church. I was so eager to move away for college! I was desperate for a fresh start and new faces. I went to a small Christian school. Only then, after some separation from my family, I realized the gravity of what transpired over the last four to five years and particularly how my dad's words had shaken my faith. It was so heavy, but I was able to find healing through Jesus's love and counseling.

Nineteen-year-old me met twenty-one-year-old him on Easter Sunday morning 2004 in church. A handsome, dapper man we will call Chad. It was the start of a beautiful friendship full of love and laughter. He made me laugh every single day. We were long-distance for the first year we dated, allowing for rich conversations from the heart. We connected deeply on a spiritual level. I admired him so much for having gone through schooling to become a pastor. He stepped away from that before finishing and started working full-time. He worked hard, loved the Lord, knew the Word, and led me well spiritually. While dating, I pressed into the Lord about our future together and it was clear. The Lord was going to use Chad to make things new in my life. We were engaged after two years. It was a fairytale! My complete dream come true.

We shared similar familial backstories, both coming from broken homes where our dads left us. In the Lord's power, we set out to break the generational curse and cycle of divorce in our families and knew when *we* married, it would be forever. We would give our children a picture of two imperfect people who loved Jesus and each other. We would be the ones who went the distance. I said "I do" in 2006 to my very best friend, and we set off into our happily ever after.

Two years into our marriage, we slammed into our first bump... Well, more of a mountain actually. He had been unfaithful. I didn't discover anything. He just told me. My soul was crushed and I felt blindsided. How could he? Why?! My first reaction, after the crying, was *of course Satan doesn't want us to make it! He wants to tear us apart!* We decided to meet with our pastor and fight for our marriage. My husband was remorseful and recommitted to me and the sanctity of our marriage. Only the Lord gave me the power to forgive and not walk away. Forgiveness was not easy at all, but it was so beautiful once we talked it out.

I'm so thankful to have walked that path of forgiveness because without it, I wouldn't have my family. Babies started coming after we had been married for seven years. Even though I had wanted babies earlier, I was so thankful to have a longer season where we built a solid marriage and developed a deeper friendship. It felt like we had the best foundation possible before bringing children into the mix. Thanks to the man who worked tirelessly to make it happen, I had the privilege of staying home with our children from the beginning. For as long as I can remember, I've wanted to be a mother. They are each such a gift and an answer to my prayers! I loved watching Chad become a dad, too. The way he celebrated all of the babies' firsts, made them laugh, and was concerned over their well-being melted my heart.

After our son turned two and our daughter was four months old, we needed to make a big cross-country move. Any move is stressful, but this one was especially so. I was dealing with undiagnosed postpartum depression. Chad was already working where we would be living and was traveling back and forth over the weekends. I was flying solo in parenting through most days and nights this season.

On the weekend of the big move, nothing went as planned. There were hold-ups with both closings. Then a call came from my dad about a small, seemingly unimportant detail about the happenings of the weekend. I was not in a location nor did I have the headspace to take this call. I asked to table the discussion until later and hurried off the phone. I got a text from him immediately afterward that forever changed our relationship. He said he was done with me and wished me a nice life. It wasn't a joke. Instead of receiving an apology in the days that followed, I got a long letter that dictated all of the reasons why he was done with our relationship. It detailed all of the ways I had disrespected him dating back to my childhood. I was heartbroken all over again. My relationship with my dad had been tumultuous ever since he left us, but this was a new low.

My husband stood by my side, comforting me as I grieved the loss of a parent who was very much still alive. The parent I had longed to have a normal relationship with for over fifteen years was willingly exiting my life, in turn, choosing to not have a relationship with his grandchildren. Chad offered me the consistency and steadiness I craved. He was God's gift to me, especially in this heavy grief. At the one-year mark of our big move, I realized Jesus had made me a new person all over again. I had forgiven my dad and was moving toward a bright future, despite that relationship not being restored.

We were involved in our local church. Chad and I were stronger than ever. I was the happiest girl in the world after finding out I was pregnant with our final baby. A sweet baby boy. After so much heartbreak, my heart grew again to love another. After he turned one, I came across the idea of picking a word or phrase for the year. It was just something to focus on in light of the cross that would help me walk out my faith daily.

> *"Abide in me, and I in you."*

Through the next few years, I chose words like "grace," "refresh," and "intentional." Coming into 2021, I had been led to the word "abide." My focus verse for the year was, *Abide in me, and I in you. As the branch cannot bear fruit by itself, unless it abides in the vine, neither can you, unless you abide in me* (John 15:4 ESV). Settling on this word was no accident as it was one of the ways I can look back now and see God's hand at work before I even knew to ask.

Enter the night that changed everything. My husband of now fourteen years came home from a long trip, but something was off, really off. My best friend refused to make eye contact with me, I barely got a peck on the cheek as a greeting, and he didn't even attempt to be with the kids. After not having been with me or the kids for two full weeks, none of these actions made sense to me. None of these were our norm. All of my alarm bells went off. The pit in my stomach grew, knowing something was really wrong. I began to pray for courage for Chad to say whatever was on his mind. I had no idea…

When we were alone, I gave him a big hug. I hoped the hug would make this nervousness go away. His eyes finally met mine. They were wild and full of fear. Suddenly, my legs felt like they were full of lead.

"What is wrong?" I asked hesitantly.

"I think I need to go to my mom's," he stated plainly.

"What? You just got home."

"Yeah, I know. That's part of the problem."

"What problem?"

"Well, I wasn't planning on saying this tonight…"

"Saying what?"

I actually don't remember exactly what he said. I think I went into shock. All I could comprehend was that he was leaving. He was not happy and couldn't do this anymore.

I don't remember much else from that night. One of our children, I couldn't even tell you which one it was, walked in seconds after he said this and immediately wanted to know why Mommy was crying. I had no words. My ears were ringing and I could feel my body involuntarily sinking. Internally, it felt like someone shut my lights off. Mercifully, Chad turned around to help get the kids ready for bed. I wondered what his answer would be to the question still lingering in the air as I retreated to the nearest quiet space, my bathroom. I looked around frantically for anything to make sense of the words I had just heard. I was freefalling.

My eyes rested on a beautiful photo on my wall that reminded me of my word of the year. *"Abide in me, and I in you."*

It felt like a safety net that caught me after falling off of a trapeze. I stared at that photo as long as humanly possible. I don't remember if I hugged my children goodnight that night. I was face to face with my absolute worst nightmare. I do remember that we had several long talks over the next couple of nights and the sentiment was the same. This was not a joke. This was not a drill. He wasn't happy and he was leaving. He insisted there was not another woman and refused to do counseling. I could feel my soul crushing under the weight of these conversations. Abandoned. Completely blindsided. How could he? Why?! What about us breaking the cycle? What about our children?

The next week was a complete blur of tears, anger, and questioning. I had asked for space to process this apart from the kids and he agreed. It was so mind-boggling that I had been dedicating my "working hours" to my kids for the last eight years and in this deep sorrow, I could barely think of them. The thought of our marriage ending consumed me. My best and closest friend didn't want to be with me anymore. He was done with me, just like my dad was.

My heart was freshly bent toward hope

We were apart for a week before we sat down again to see if anything had changed. Indeed, he had not changed his mind. It was over. It was clear he had already researched the process of getting a divorce. That night would be the night he moved out, and the first night I saw him cry in all of this. I asked him to tell the kids he was leaving. He was upset because they didn't understand. *Well, of course, they don't get it! Why would their daddy not want to live with them?!* I just stared at him, stupefied. Where do you stand when your husband is packing his bags to leave his family? What do you do? I've never felt more useless or helpless in my life.

After another week of processing him actually being gone and learning new rhythms of being a single mom, I had some reflective time and wondered what part I had in all of this going array. After some precious alone time with the Lord, He gently allowed me to see that I had placed my marriage and my husband on a pedestal. How can a God-ordained marriage become an idol? Just like anything else. By placing too much importance in something other than the Lord. I took pride in, even bordering on arrogance, how solid our marriage was and how we could be a shining example for others in a sea of so many divorces. While having a great marriage is amazing, I allowed my husband to be first in my heart... before God. I spent more time planning date nights and weekend getaways with Chad than prayer or affections toward the Lord. I cherished Chad first and foremost and, while I loved the Lord, admittedly He was a bit of an afterthought. I knew I was wrong for that and was humbled. I leveled with Jesus and prayed, "Please be first in my life again. You really are all I need. All anyone needs." The sweet song "Jireh" was playing as this sin was revealed in my heart. "I'll never be more loved than I am right now."[2] It was a perfect reminder that no matter how I messed up, God would always love me.

My heart was freshly bent toward hope, and I began praying for our marriage to be restored, if that was God's will. More than anything else, I was praying the Lord would bring to light what was being done in the darkness. This sudden separation still just made no sense to me. It simply didn't add up; however, tomorrow held so much promise. I was packing for a preplanned trip with my mom, brother, and sister. We were heading to St. Thomas in the U.S. Virgin Islands! What provisional timing for a trip like this!

I was excitedly packing until I got a phone call that evening that changed everything. What was done in darkness came to light in an instant.

"Rachel?" The unknown caller's voice was a man's.

"Yes...?" I reluctantly replied.

"You're married to Chad? You have three kids?"

I was terrified. "Who is this?!"

"Well, you should make sure the kids are in another room and you should sit down."

The other woman's husband was on the other end of the line. He had found their secret messages and explained their indiscretions. While this explained everything, I still couldn't grasp that this was my reality. Again?! How could Chad do this?! Why?! And why not just tell me *she* was the reason he was leaving?! Once I had heard enough to get the picture, I immediately hung up.

Now I knew it was really over. Completely dead. My soul was crushed and I was abandoned again, only this time, I had been had. I was a fool. How could I have possibly believed him when he said there was no one else? My soul was crushed. I thought two weeks ago held the worst night of my life. No, it was now. I couldn't stand. My knees buckled underneath me and I hit the floor. Adrenaline was rushing through my veins, but oddly I had no strength. There was a hollowing happening in my head that made me feel faint. My gag reflex started going haywire. No warning or forethought. I hadn't even eaten that day, but my body was undone. I wasn't even nauseous, but I couldn't stop gagging. I had locked myself in my room during the call and texted my dear friend. She came and got the kids immediately. I could not be responsible for them now. My body was overcome, and I didn't recognize this physical and emotional reaction. I had had panic attacks before, but this was way past that. I had never been in such a low place. The shadow of death was threatening me. It physically hurt to breathe. I thought my chest would just cave in completely. Was I going to die from the pain of this betrayal? I honestly wondered if I would live another day to see my kids again. God help me.

I'm not sure how it happened, but my house was full of my support system pretty soon. People who cared for and loved me surrounded me, but somehow I still felt so alone. They hurt for me and empathized with me, but no one else seemed to be familiar with my pain. As my friends and family went to work to help me get my footing, taking down any photos of him, changing locks, researching attorneys, I couldn't stay focused on any one thing. The only thing that brought me comfort that night was singing "Jireh." I played it on repeat so many times that my aunt even questioned, "Seriously? This song again?" But singing these lyrics back to the one who knew this day was coming somehow brought peace to my aching soul.

"Going through a storm but I won't go down
I hear Your voice
Carried in the rhythm of the wind to call me out
You would cross an ocean so I wouldn't drown
You've never been closer than You are right now
You are Jireh, You are enough"[3]

I was clinging to these words and the hope of not actually drowning. I was dying to hear the Lord's voice in this moment. The water was up to my neck and threatening to take me under, but I knew He wouldn't let me drown. He had a plan. He was enough for me. I could remember the pinprick of light and hope from Russ's words the week before. "I know it feels like you're freefalling, but because you have Jesus, He won't let you fall all the way down. He's already caught you and will carry you through this."

it would be a delicate balance of grieving while staying surrendered and not picking up bitterness along the way.

See, y'all. It was no accident that I had a sweet, quiet time with the Lord just hours before this phone call. My heart was already in a different space from that intimate time with Him. He's a good Shepherd and knows just what His sheep need. I needed to know the truth about the reasons behind my husband's leaving. I needed to know it was over. After the first time, trust was hard enough to rebuild. I knew there wouldn't be another chance. There would be no options for reconciliation. From here on out, it would be a delicate balance of grieving while staying surrendered and not picking up bitterness along the way.

As I lay in bed that night, I was still spinning in my living nightmare. My mind began to click things into place, like my oldest telling me a few months prior right in front of his dad, "Mom, Dad has been talking to another girl. I saw their text messages." I remembered how quickly Chad chastised him about making up stories like that. My mind continued to spin, but internally, somehow I was more at peace. I only found sleep by listening to "Whole Heart" by Hillsong and imagining being held by my Father.

"Hold me now
In the hands that created the heavens
Find me now
Where the grace runs as deep as Your scars
You pulled me from the clay
You set me on a rock
Called me by Your Name
And made my heart whole again
Lifted up
And my knees know it's all for Your glory
That I might stand
With more reasons to sing than to fear
You pulled me from the clay
Set me on a rock
Called me by Your Name
And made my heart whole again
So here I stand
High in surrender
I need You now"[4]

Even though my future felt so unsure, I knew I could rest in the Lord and His plan. I prayed, "Father, make my heart whole again." I knew He would see me through this mess. I would need to grieve all that was, our dreams, and what could have been, but at that moment, I had more reasons to sing than to fear. I was reminded of His heart for His children.

*"For I know the plans I have for you," declares the Lord,
"plans to prosper you and not to harm you, plans to give
you hope and a future."* Jeremiah 29:11 (NIV)

The next day still held much promise. I had never needed to be with my family so much. I needed their looks of understanding without saying any words and their vulnerability of crying with me. The Lord knew I would need that warm sun on my face to help dry my tears. Then to just *be* with my siblings. Without fail, we would get stupid silly and laugh so hard it became an ab workout! It was the best way to hit the pause button on all of the chaos happening back home.

Aside from sobbing on my brother's shoulder all the way through security, the flight there was hardly remarkable. I spent most of it lying in my mom's lap weeping while she stroked my hair. We had a very sweet flight attendant, Maggie, who took amazing care of us. She seemed to understand the heartbreak I was in and was empathetic. After chatting for a bit with my family, we realized she would be the flight attendant for our return flight, as well! She was excited she would be able to see us again, as were we.

While we were in St. Thomas, we lived our best lives soaking up the sun, swimming in turquoise waters, and watching incredible sunsets. We took a boat over to St. John to snorkel at a couple of popular spots, including the Virgin Island National Park. We swam with sea turtles and all sorts of colorful fish. We were filled with wonder and adventure. Ten out of ten would recommend catching the sunset while on a boat with the mountains in the distance!

The Lord tended to my shattered heart while we were there, escaping from my reality. I gave myself permission to grieve as much as I needed, even if it meant less quality time with my family. I spent many hours crying while sitting on random docks with my feet in the water and watched the ocean carry away my tears. Knowing my family wasn't far away was so comforting. I tried to imagine life without my husband, but that felt impossible, so I would just grieve more. In those moments, I knew Jesus was sitting with me, hurting with me.

We ended our trip with a Mother's Day brunch overlooking the water. I was repurposed and rejuvenated somewhat. I was ready to be back with my children. I knew once I was back with them, I would need to explain a bit more that their dad was not coming back home. This was our new reality and the kids needed to understand.

We were all happy to see Maggie's familiar face on the return flight. Once we got settled in and headed back to the States, Maggie came to me with a gift in hand. "In all my years as a flight attendant, I've never given a passenger a gift. But you've stuck with me, and I felt like I should." Opening the card, the only thing on the front was a rainbow. Cue the tears. The Lord has used rainbows over the years to speak His promises back to me. How would Maggie know that? Inside she wrote, "Rachel, treat yourself well! Look for the rainbow after the storm!" The Lord used Maggie that day to speak life over my storm and it reminded me that He was always with me. There would be beauty again after this.

> *What a picture of how Jesus is with us. He knows the bad things coming our way and is there with quiet, strong comfort.*

As our plane flew over the Caribbean Ocean, storm clouds gathered in the distance and I contemplated the anatomy of a rainbow. Rainbows need water, most often rain, to pass through and then reflect, refract, and disperse light into a beautiful bow of colors. We know Jesus is the Light of the World, so I couldn't help but see the spiritual parallel in my own storm. He could use my current storm to greater reflect His light in my life. I was encouraged the Light of the World could use this awful hurricane I was weathering and turn it into something beautiful. From that moment on, I would never be able to see rainbows at face value.

Once we landed in the States, I was reunited with my sweet babies. With such provision as only the Lord could provide, I didn't have to have this heart-wrenching conversation between myself and my children about our new family dynamic alone. My immediate family was also able to be present. My kids were surrounded by their loved ones while they received this terrible news. My kids got to see their grandmother, aunt, and uncle all cry with them and received comfort from those intimately acquainted with their pain. What a picture of how Jesus is with us. He knows the bad things coming our way and is there with quiet, strong comfort. Just like Jehovah Jireh, He had already provided time and space for this conversation to happen so that my children weren't alone.

When I returned back home with my kids in tow, we got back to our rhythms. The very next morning, I was doing devotions and journaling. My ADHD-self got distracted, but the next time I passed by my still-open Bible, a scripture immediately caught my eye.

> *"Do not be afraid; you will not be put to shame. Do not fear disgrace; you will not be humiliated. You will forget the shame of your youth and remember no more the reproach of your widowhood. For your Maker is your husband—the Lord Almighty is his name— the Holy One of Israel is your Redeemer; he is called the God of all the earth. The Lord will call you back as if you were a wife deserted and distressed in spirit— a wife who married young, only to be rejected," says your God. "For a brief moment I abandoned you, but with deep compassion I will bring you back... Though the mountains be shaken and the hills be removed, yet my unfailing love for you will not be shaken nor my covenant of peace be removed," says the Lord, who has compassion on you.* Isaiah 54:4 -7,10 (NIV)

Wait, what?! I knew this chapter! Eighteen years before this, the Lord got me up one night in college to read this exact chapter! I had *no* idea what it meant at the time and got nervous after reading the first verse. "*Sing, barren woman, you who never bore a child; burst into song, shout for joy, you who were never in labor; because more are the children of the desolate woman than of her who has a husband," says the Lord* (NIV). I thought it meant I was not going to have children, and it frightened me because I had only ever wanted to be a mother!

I tucked this chapter away in my heart all those years ago. Surely it meant something if He led me to it, but back then it was just a mystery. When I first found this passage, it was six months before I met Chad.

Now, eighteen years later, I just couldn't believe what I was reading! It described me perfectly in that moment. "Okay, Lord. You are my Maker and my Husband. You knew this would happen. You told me eighteen years ago. You are here with me and have redeemed me. You will redeem this situation. Your unfailing love for me will not be shaken."

> *My husband leaving didn't just happen to me, but the good God would bring from this happened for me.*

Little did I know this was just the beginning…

The Lord would repeatedly prove to me His hand was sovereignly overseeing my life. Not just during our separation, leading up to the inevitable divorce, but everything that had happened in my life up until this point was not an accident. It was preparation for seasons to come. My husband leaving didn't just happen *to* me, but the good God would bring from this happened *for* me. I know, it sounds crazy.

I would be honored to share some of the lessons I've learned along the way over the last two years. Faith-anchoring lessons. Things that must be written down because our simple human minds so quickly forget God's goodness in our lives, but also so crazy they would be hard to believe. But ultimately, because of how Paul said it best,

> *Praise be to the God and Father of our Lord Jesus Christ,*
> *the Father of compassion and the God of all comfort, who*

comforts us in all our troubles, so that we can comfort those in any trouble with the comfort we ourselves receive from God. For just as we share abundantly in the sufferings of Christ, so also our comfort abounds through Christ. If we are distressed, it is for your comfort and salvation; if we are comforted, it is for your comfort, which produces in you patient endurance of the same sufferings we suffer. And our hope for you is firm, because we know that just as you share in our sufferings, so also you share in our comfort. 2 Corinthians 1:3-7 (NIV)

These verses are my prayer. That the comfort I have received is passed on to you. That your walk with the Lord will deepen as you begin to see His hand in your suffering. Or if you don't know Him at all, that you would have a glimpse of how the Father sees you. You are redeemed. You are deeply loved and cherished. Your tears matter.

You are redeemed. You are deeply loved and cherished. Your tears matter.

Reflection

- Think about your own story. What broken promises have you experienced?

- Allow the Holy Spirit to bring an area of brokenness to your mind. I believe He wants to heal you and redeem that situation.

Heavenly Father, thank you so much for Your sovereign hand in my life. Thank you for Your goodness and mercy that follow me everywhere I go. You are so good to me. Even when met with the darkest of situations, may I seek Your face. I ask that You give me eyes to see how You're moving in my life. In turn, may I faithfully bear Your light to a world in need of a Savior. Amen.

CHAPTER 2
Unwanted Weeds of the Heart

Forgiveness is such a weighty word. We know we should forgive, the big things and even the small things. But why and how? Well, Jesus says it for one thing, but does it release the other person from what they've done and the consequences? No. There are always natural consequences for anything you do, good or otherwise. That's got to be a law of science, right?

A couple of months into our separation, I realized I was becoming bitter. Of course, I was rightfully still hurt and angry, but I felt nasty inside. My anger had crossed over from righteous anger to more of a sinful anger where I really just wanted Chad to suffer like I was. I wanted God to make him pay, to take His vengeance, to enact His swift justice. I could keep on this way, but I knew deep down it wasn't productive.

I watched the movie *War Room* for the first time. The way the little old lady, Mrs. Clara, was ministering to Elizabeth, the younger, upset wife struck me. I felt the Lord's conviction press on my heart. Mrs. Clara said, "Elizabeth, it comes down to this: Jesus shed His blood on the cross. He died for you, even when you did not deserve it. And He rose from the grave and offers forgiveness and salvation for anyone who turns to Him. But the Bible also says that we can't ask Him to forgive us while refusing to forgive others."

I knew immediately I had to begin walking that out. This was not my first rodeo in walking out forgiveness related to trauma, deceit, or abandonment, so I remembered it was not an overnight phenomenon, but a process. The process of forgiving my dad took years. I would forgive, then something new would happen that was traumatic. That cycle repeated until that fateful text from him that ended our relationship. As hard as it was, it allowed me to jump off of the roller coaster of a toxic relationship and allow for real, true healing. Even then forgiveness still took time, especially since there was no repentance.

When it came to Chad, I began with a prayer asking for help to forgive and to maintain a heart posture of forgiveness. I would never be able to forgive him in my own strength. I would need a makeover of the heart by the Holy Spirit.

> *Even then forgiveness still took time, especially since there was no repentance.*

> *Make every effort to live in peace with everyone and to be holy; without holiness, no one will see the Lord. See to it that no one falls short of the grace of God and that no bitter root grows up to cause trouble and defile many.*
> Hebrews 12:14-15 (NIV)

Scripture tells us once you become bitter, you end up becoming a hindrance to other people and their walk with the Lord, as well. I don't know about you, but I'd prefer not to be a hindrance or trip anyone else up. I don't want to be the reason for someone's heart being poisoned and missing God's grace, especially not those three tiny faces I was caring for. Discipling my children's hearts had always been a top priority. Remembering this alone was enough motivation to make sure I dealt with any root of bitterness in my heart.

Not surprisingly with the timing, Lysa TerKeurst came out with a book on the subject of forgiveness titled *Forgiving What You Can't Forget*. Can I just go off on a tangent for a sec? God's timing, y'all! It is not a coincidence! Throughout this season, it's hit me over and over that, for the most part, there really are no such things as coincidences. More like perfectly timed winks from our heavenly Father. Okay, back to Lysa. She was featured in Jennie Allen's *Made for This* podcast I listened to just a couple of days after watching *War Room*. Lysa said,

> "Forgiveness is two parts. Forgiveness is both a decision and it's a process. You make the decision to forgive for the fact of what happened, but then you can walk through the longer process of healing for forgiving for the impact that this has had on you. For every wound, there is a fact, and there's an impact. There's the fact of what happened and the impact of how this has affected you, how much this cost you emotionally. Isn't it interesting that the Bible calls what we need to forgive other people of- those offenses, those hurts, the emotional cost of it all- Jesus himself refers to all of that hurt as debt. It's emotional debt, and it is OK to make the decision to forgive and still need to walk through the process of forgiving."[5]

The concept of emotional debt took me time to process. I had to face the facts of all of the ways my husband broke our marital covenant. There were things I did know about and things I would find out later, but there was so much more fallout than just the marriage. Watching the kids cry for their dad to be present was unbearable. The events that he missed. The kids' nightly bedtime routine missed. More heartbreak. Watching the little ones cry because Mommy was crying was excruciating. This was all emotional debt and cost our family tremendously. I'm not even sure there will ever be an end to the emotional debt this side of heaven.

the Lord allowed me to see my husband as God did.

19

In the days following, the Lord allowed me to see my husband as God did. A lost child, tied up in bondage because he had bought into the deception and lies of the Enemy. When you're trapped in darkness, you don't know which way is up. I don't know how many affairs he had over the course of our marriage, and ultimately, it doesn't matter. It all had to be forgiven just the same.

Shortly thereafter, I felt a strong conviction. I needed to tell my husband, in kindness, that I was working on forgiving him. I wrestled with a bunch of questions about this. Did he deserve forgiveness when he hadn't even apologized? While he continued to deny his affair, no less! Did he deserve kindness from me? Did he need to know anything about my own convictions or walk with the Lord? The Spirit challenged me to flip that. Do any of us deserve kindness or forgiveness? That's a hard no. We're all so full of sin and unrighteous thoughts and behaviors. Our righteousness, even on our best days,

> *I was free, having let go of my bitterness that would only eat me alive.*

is as filthy rags. We will never be holy or worthy on our own… but Jesus. He steps in and offers forgiveness and atonement for anything we've ever done. How, then, can we not turn around and offer that same forgiveness to those who have done us wrong, even in the absence of remorse?

I knew I would have the opportunity to see him later when exchanging the kids. I thought about it all day. I talked myself out of it seventeen times and even had a couple of friends tell me not to do it, but I had been walking with the Lord long enough to know that you don't ignore His promptings. I had to do it. What on earth to say, though? I was confident the Spirit would give me the words to say. At the end of the night, I came out to the driveway, once the kids had gone inside, and recited to Chad,

You are always and dearly loved by God!…Be merciful as you endeavor to understand others, and be compassionate, showing kindness toward all. Be gentle and humble, unoffendable in your patience with others. Tolerate the weaknesses of those in the family of faith, forgiving one another in the same way you have been graciously forgiven by Jesus Christ. If you find fault with someone, release this same gift of forgiveness to them. Colossians 3:12-13 (TPT)

I then told him, "That said, I just wanted to let you know I'm working on forgiving you for everything. Leaving us. The affair. All of it."

I probably will never know on this side of eternity why I was so convicted to say anything that particular night. I mean, you can forgive someone, and you don't have to make an announcement about it. Then again, I've learned that it's futile to question God's timing. What I do know is that the man who received those words looked super surprised and appreciative to receive a kind word. Chad was reminded from the verses I recited that God dearly loved him, and there will never be a downside to that. I also know that once I had been obedient, I was able to walk back inside with my babies feeling so light and free!

Forgiveness is never easy and is always our choice

This didn't let him off the hook for his natural consequences. Those would still happen whether either of us wanted them to or not. But I was free, having let go of my bitterness that would only eat me alive. And that's exactly what forgiveness does. It surrenders your need for consequences to the Lord. We can trust He'll take care of the consequences however is best.

Hear me out: I'm a plant girl. Bitterness is like a disease or a gnarly weed, and it has the power to overtake our hearts if left unchecked. Weeds can literally choke out the healthy growth in your yard. Beginning to walk out a heart rooted in forgiveness allowed that bitterness not to get any more attention, or sun, and die off just like weeds sprayed with weed killer.

In fact, Eugene Peterson, author of *The Message*, said it like this.

> *Work at getting along with each other and with God.*
> *Otherwise you'll never get so much as a glimpse of God.*
> *Make sure no one gets left out of God's generosity. Keep*
> *a sharp eye out for weeds of bitter discontent. A thistle*
> *or two gone to seed can ruin a whole garden in no time.*
> Hebrews 12:14-15 (MSG)

Forgiveness is never easy and is always our choice, but it's so freeing, and I believe it is one of the first steps toward real healing.

Again, as Lysa so eloquently explains, forgiveness isn't a one-time thing, but a decision and then a process of letting go of the emotional debt. Ultimately, it's allowing the Lord to deal with them while not weighing down your own heart.

Reflection

- Have you ever struggled to forgive someone who badly hurt you?

- Take an honest look at the landscape of your heart. Is there bitterness hiding out that needs to be surrendered?

- What steps can you take today to begin walking out forgiveness?

Dear Jesus, thank you for shedding Your innocent blood in my place. Thank you for forgiving me and for Your love that covers a multitude of sins. Help me to forgive as You forgive. Help bitterness not grow rampant in my heart, but soften my heart toward those who have deeply hurt me. Help me make every effort to live at peace with those who hurt me. Help me surrender the punishment I may think they are deserving to Your just and capable hands. Amen.

CHAPTER 3
Storms Don't Last Forever

In the early days of Chad leaving us, even before the topic of for-giveness came up, I could hear my former boss in my head saying, "Rachel, hope is not a strategy!" I hadn't heard this phrase in nearly a decade, but it was pestering me and dashing any smidgen of hope I had left in my heart. While this phrase might be true in sales, it was a fiery arrow from the Enemy piercing my heart and threatening to take down my faith. What was I hoping for? I'm not even sure. Reconciliation? My husband to wake up from this nightmare he put us in? That the Lord would step in with holy justice and righteous vengeance righting all the wrongs done to me? Maybe just some normalcy?

I'll be honest, in those early days of just finding out all of the horren-dous details of the affair, my only "hope" was for God to rain down holy fire on their heads, as awful as that sounds. How could they deserve to go unpunished, living a shiny new amazing life of bliss, leaving me and our three kids in the dust? It wasn't fair. But hoping for my husband to have any harsh consequences ultimately proved fruitless and a complete waste of energy. The Lord promises to take vengeance in His own way on His own timetable.

All I know is that "hope is not a strategy" rolled around in my head for far too long! Isn't hope a cornerstone of the Christian faith? I had to go on a journey to re-teach myself what hope was and what it was not. I needed to re-learn its importance and ways I could walk it out. I dove headfirst into the Word to see what I could find.

Faith shows the reality of what we hope for; it is the evidence of things we cannot see. Hebrews 11:1 (NLT)

Oh, okay, but that wasn't enough. I needed more evidence. I had known this verse my whole life, but I was just not getting it right now. A broken heart is a fickle thing!

That is why we labor and strive, because we have put our hope in the living God, who is the Savior of all people, and especially of those who believe. 1 Timothy 4:10 (NIV)

Those who hope in me will not be disappointed. Isaiah 49:23 (NIV)

Hmmm, so you say. My life was a pile of disappointments. I certainly never *hoped* this would happen. I believed and was massively disappointed. I needed something more concrete.

Israel, put your hope in the Lord, for with the Lord is unfailing love and with him is full redemption. Psalm 130:7 (NIV)

Redemption? Really? Now, that's a word I can get on board with. Can God redeem my story?

Therefore, we who have fled to him for refuge can have great confidence as we hold to the hope that lies before us. This hope is a strong and trustworthy anchor for our souls. Hebrews 6:18-19 (NLT)

Wow! Now I was getting it! I needed this unshakeable hope, this strength and comfort. So, what exactly is hope? It's not wishful thinking. It's not an abstract expectation of something good. It's a belief in the promises of God and an eager expectation of seeing the promises ful-filled. Hope was bigger than me and my situation. Every single one of our trials and seasons of suffering leads us back to this.

> *Not only so, but we also glory in our sufferings, because we know that suffering produces perseverance; perseverance, character; and character, hope. And hope does not put us to shame, because God's love has been poured out into our hearts through the Holy Spirit, who has been given to us.* Romans 5:3-5 (NIV)

In our suffering, heartbreaks, and brokenness, we learn what true hope is at a deeper level. We can know in full confidence that it will not put us to shame. Hope does not disappoint us.

> *But the eyes of the Lord are on those who fear him, on those whose hope is in his unfailing love,* Psalm 33:18 (NIV)

His unfailing love. His mercy. Grace. His loving kindness. Compassion. His everlasting covenant toward us. The Hebrew word for all of these is "hesed," a new "h" word I learned.[6] I love that Wikipedia says it's not a word easily translated into English[7]. Then again, His love is really too much for us to ever truly fathom. Yet, the verse above reminds us that His hesed *is* worth putting our hope in. This is why we can have assurance that our hope in Him will never be misplaced. His covenantal love will always chase us down.

His covenantal love will always chase us down.

After my research on hope, I replaced the narrative of "hope is not a strategy" to the sweet words of CeCe Winans's song "Believe For It." Ultimately, I can have hope now and forever because there is an empty grave as this legendary singer belted out,

"We know that hope is never lost
For there is still an empty grave
God we believe no matter what
There is power in Your name"[8]

A few words that stood out to me in this study, looking at various Bible translations were unshakeable, unfailing, joyful confidence, an unbreakable anchor holding ourselves to God. No wonder I had lost hope. All of these words describing hope had been tampered with. Even though I would consider my faith pretty strong, I realized my hope wasn't unshakeable because this sudden separation rocked me to my core. The ground beneath me shook as I watched my husband walk away. Hope is supposed to be unfailing, but I felt I somehow failed. My marriage failed. I no longer had a joyful confidence, try as I might. But here is where the strength of the Lord comes in. When we are in a relationship with Him, He is our anchor, and we are forever tethered to the Lord. He's the solid anchor we can lean back against on dark days like these and let Him do the heavy lifting. If we are tethered and resting in Him, the true unbreakable Anchor, we can't help but have a joyful confidence. It comes in the peace that He provides.

After I had completed my Word study on hope, my brother had a vision, and I share it with his permission. It really is such a beautiful image of what God does with our brokenness, not just mine, and brings purpose to the pain so that we can reach others. I certainly haven't always been this "jar" in this season, but it is the absolute best case scenario for all of this pain. I believe this is how He receives glory in the midst of our pain.

"I'm watching you remain held together where most would expect your jar to be shattered and scattered on the ground. I'm seeing the jar of your life – your identity as a daughter of God, woman, mom, sister, and friend – grafted together by the love of Jesus. I think of communion and how His body was broken for us so ours wouldn't have to be. Because of that, your jar is whole and His Spirit can dwell in that jar. The jar holds life, hope, encouragement, faith, and love. Then I see your jar tip over and pour out those attributes to your kids, friends, and community. It's an endless cycle of Him pouring into that jar fresh and new Spirit, like water, and transferring it obediently in a state of overflow to others so He can do it over and over again."

I also received hope again in a different way. A hope of a brand new future. Along the journey of the separation, I sought out refuge with a couple of different girlfriends who loved the Lord. I'd visit them to escape my reality, but Jesus, in His loving kindness, always met me there. Isn't that just how it goes when Jesus is your friendships' common denominator? During these visits, I noticed the husbands would initiate devotional times with the children at bedtime. I was blown away! Even as a child, I was not being led by my dad; I was

> *The night has endured for a long time, but the morning is here.*

responsible for my own spiritual disciplines. Fast forward to being a parent, unbeknownst to me, I had been the one spiritual leader for my children throughout their lives. I didn't know it could be any different. I truly didn't realize men could have this kind of initiative, this kind of care for helping their children grow spiritually and in the Word. I witnessed humble men, who legitimately cared about the concerns of their kids' day, the way their children would grow their knowledge in the Word, and most importantly, they led their children by example.

In these moments, this revelation opened my mind to what life would be like with someone who loved the Lord and cared enough to share that with their children. I had a new hope. It was the beginning of a new spark. A new desire. A new thought to pray for whenever I would be ready to entertain the idea of dating. A new possibility of a better and richer life in Christ. A new sense of optimism and feeling hopeful about a beautiful future. A new peace that God would not waste all this pain.

Let us draw near to God with a sincere heart and with the full assurance that faith brings, having our hearts sprinkled to cleanse us from a guilty conscience and having our bodies washed with pure water. Let us hold unswervingly to the hope we profess, for he who promised is faithful. And let us consider how we may spur one another on toward love and good deeds, not giving up meeting together, as some are in the habit of doing, but encouraging one another— and all the more as you see the Day approaching. Hebrews 10:22-25 (NIV)

Hope continues to evolve in my heart as time passes. I'm constantly reminded of the promises of God. One that keeps coming up is Psalm 126:5. *Those who sow with tears will reap with songs of joy.* I have hope that my time of grief and weeping is over. Not only is it over, but God is making all things new. He won't allow this time to be a waste, but has promised to turn this into a time of joy! There will be joy in the morning! The night has endured for a long time, but the morning is here. The fact is that God sees our pain and hurts when we hurt. He longs to comfort us. I wholeheartedly believe He has collected all of my tears and intends to use them to further His kingdom.

> *I must have hope and a firm belief that Christ will redeem all of this pain.*

"Great is Thy faithfulness, O God my Father;
There is no shadow of turning with Thee;
Thou changest not, Thy compassions, they fail not;
As Thou hast been, Thou forever will be.
Great is Thy faithfulness!
Great is Thy faithfulness!
Morning by morning new mercies I see.
All I have needed thy hand hath provided;

Great is Thy faithfulness, Lord, unto me!"
-"Great Is Thy Faithfulness," Hymn

His mercies are new every morning. He's ready and waiting with a steady hand to offer grace to start again. Every new day is a fresh opportunity to be in the secret place with the Savior and see the new things He's doing through you and around you. I feel the Lord has spoken this verse over me on so many occasions that it has begun to feel like my anthem. *Forget the former things; do not dwell on the past. See, I am doing a new thing! Now it springs up; do you not perceive it? I am making a way in the wilderness and streams in the wasteland* (Isa. 43:18-19 NIV). It's a command to stop looking backward and a promise that makes me excited about what's coming. It's a charge to no longer ruminate on the hurricane-force storm I had just been through, but an invitation to find the beautiful rainbow shining through the raindrops. It's the epitome of hope.

It's no secret that the life of a single mom is hard. This is another area I've had to preach hope back to my own heart. Without having anyone else to speak into my children's life consistently, I'm reminded of my single biggest mission right now, my kids' hearts. I've been graciously entrusted with them and must steward them well. It's my honor to equip them and point them to Christ. If I can't regularly, who will? Even though I am tired and weary most days, I must have hope and a firm belief that Christ will redeem all of this pain. Not only for myself, but I need to hold onto hope for the sake of my children, as well. Sometimes they get fed up with our new family dynamic and the hardships that come along with it. It's my privilege to teach them about what hope is and who our hope is found in. They, too, have started to dream about what the future may hold for our family.

Reflection

- Have you ever felt hopeless? How did you find hope once again?

- What was your favorite part of the word study on hope? What areas of your heart need to have the message of hope preached to it?

- Ask the Father to bring someone in your life to mind who might need to hear the message of hope right now. How are you being led to reach out to them?

Father God, thank you for taking me on a gentle journey to remind me of what hope is and what hope is not. Thank you for being my ultimate source of hope. Even through life's trials and hard seasons, help me hold fast to unshakeable hope like a strong, unbreakable anchor that holds my soul to You. May I maintain a joyful confidence because of what You have done for me and lean into Your promises of hope, never disappointing me. Lord, use my broken situation to shine Your hope and truth to a dying world. Thank you in advance for redeeming my story! Amen.

CHAPTER 4

A Sunset With the Gardener

T he Bible says God prunes those who love Him. Pruning makes room for more growth in the future. Pruning is painful and, at the same time, absolutely necessary to grow in step with Him. Pruning is not a punishment, but an honor. I had been nearly a year into our separation when the Lord spoke to me about this. I felt a sense of urgency to get alone with the Lord because He had something to say. I went to a beautiful, wide-open field just in time to watch a gorgeous sunset unfold. I opened my Bible to John 15, the passage that held my word for the year "abide."

> *I am the true vine, and my Father is the vinedresser. Every branch in me that does not bear fruit he takes away, and every branch that does bear fruit he prunes, that it may bear more fruit. Already you are clean because of the word that I have spoken to you. Abide in me, and I in you. As the branch cannot bear fruit by itself, unless it abides in the vine, neither can you, unless you abide in me. I am the vine; you are the branches. Whoever abides in me and I in him, he it is that bears much fruit, for apart from me you can do nothing. If anyone does not abide in me he is thrown away like a branch and withers; and the branches are gathered, thrown into the fire, and burned.*
> John 15:1-6 (ESV)

I heard the Lord speak to my heart, "I cut him from you. I am the best Gardener." *Wait. What, Lord? What do You mean? Why would You do that? You say You value marriage. What about marriage being a sacred covenant?!* I had so many questions.

"Abide in me and I in you." The Gardener is the only one who knows which branch is viable and which branches are dead with no chance of survival or restoration. Only God really knows Chad's heart. Only God knows how he treated our marriage covenant. Only the Gardener knows my husband's heart toward me. Even well after Chad left, I continued to learn about instances he had been unfaithful to me. The Lord was slowly and ever so gently opening my eyes to the fact that because of Chad's continual sin, our marriage was, in fact, dead. Why would a good Gardener allow a dead branch to stay attached?

> *The Gardener is the only one who knows which branch is viable and which branches are dead with no chance of survival or restoration.*

Continuing to observe the ever-changing sky, I kept reading.

> *You did not choose me, but I chose you and appointed you that you should go and bear fruit and that your fruit should abide, so that whatever you ask the Father in my name, he may give it to you.* John 15:16 (ESV)

Again, I heard God speak. "I chose you, Rachel. I have appointed you to go and bear fruit, fruit that will last." Is it possible that I would be able to bear the same fruit if the dead branch of my marriage was still present? Was I bearing the fruit the Father wanted me to toward the end of our marriage? I don't believe I was.

My head was spinning with questions, but I was at peace. Now, the sky was a breathtaking gradient of oranges, pinks, purples, and blues.

Half of the clouds in the sky nearly resembled a rainbow. I beheld His glory in that moment.

I walked away from that moment… processing. That was *a lot*. I would need wise counsel to help me fully understand what the Lord was saying. But as things became clear, it was so evident that all of this was working together for my good. The soul crushing, heartbreaking pain was for my good, and ultimately for His glory. I knew I could trust in the promise that He would restore all that the Enemy stole from me during this time.

Months later, I received even more clarity on this from a friend. My girlfriend read me a quote from Elisabeth Elliot. "The life of the vine is strengthened in one part while another part's being cut away…The sun reaches places it could not have reached before."[9] Here we go again with God's impeccable timing.

My planty girl self had to let this one marinate. I know that the plant is strengthened when specific parts are cut back, and usually, the plant comes back better than before it was cut. But what was such an epiphany to me is that the sun can reach parts of the plant that it had never touched before. The sun is the lifeline for a plant. Without sunlight, a plant cannot thrive. If the plant is in darkness for too long, it won't survive. And that is the same for the lower branches, or in the case of humans, the callings, giftings, or talents that we have. Have you heard the analogy that humans are basically just complex houseplants? We need sun, water, and care just like a plant. No doubt that's true physically, but spiritually all the more, and all of that is found in one Gardener, who is the Living Water.

> I could trust in the promise that He would restore all that the Enemy stole from me during this time.

It's not lost on me that He didn't say, "I cut him from you," right after my husband left. Not even a couple of months after he left, but nearly a year. I had nearly a year to wrap my mind around the fact that my marriage was over before I would find out that it was all very intentional. He is a gentle Father and to have learned this newfound truth early on, I don't know what I would've done. I honestly think I would've been tempted to turn from God and shut Him out. As it was, He knew I was strong enough to hear this at this particular point, after time had passed and some grief had been worked through.

Does God cause bad things in our lives to happen? No, I don't believe He does. Does He allow them? Absolutely. I believe I would have found out about the extramarital relationships one way or another, but it was God's mercy that gave my husband the courage to tell me that initial night he was putting an end to our marriage. I remember that pivotal night he said he had not intended on telling me right then, but a couple of hours beforehand, I had prayed for him to be filled with courage and say whatever was on his mind. I really do think it was so merciful the way it played out.

Does God cause bad things in our lives to happen? No, I don't believe He does. Does He allow them? Absolutely.

Just a little side note of encouragement. Do I think my ex-husband is beyond the grasp of the Lord's reach? No, not at all. While the Lord may have cut him from me and our marriage, that doesn't mean it's not possible for him to be in a right relationship with God. Here are Paul's words regarding branches that have been broken off:

> Consider therefore the kindness and sternness of God: sternness to those who fell, but kindness to you, provided that you continue in his kindness. Otherwise, you also will be cut off. And if they do not persist in unbelief, they will be grafted in, for God is able to graft them in again. After all, if you were cut out of an olive tree that is wild by nature, and contrary to nature were grafted into a cultivated olive tree, how much more readily will these,

the natural branches, be grafted into their own olive tree!
Romans 11:22-24 (NIV)

So, I pray for him often to be grafted back in to the vine and in right relationship with the Father. I believe with my whole heart that one day he will be.

On the other hand, I believe the good Gardener pruned my marriage, or my idol, from me not just because He knew Chad's heart, but He knew mine, too. He knew that I was far too dependent on and idolized my husband. I looked to him for so many things, leaving not much room for the Lord. I cherished spending quality time with Chad so much. Of course, having quality time together is good and right for marriage, but the quality time I was dedicating to spending with the Lord was insufficient. My husband had my time, attention, and affections. God did, too, but so much less of them. Having anything as an idol creates a barrier between you and God which is never okay. Pastor Dave Furman said, "Suffering is a prime time for the revelation of the idols in our hearts,"[10] and I couldn't agree more.

As hard as it is to say, I'm thankful for this awful mess because, in the end, it drew me close to the heart of the Father. My idol, the thing I worshiped more than Christ, was revealed in my husband's leaving.

"God isn't causing this [pain and suffering]; he's allowing it. God isn't picking on us. He's handpicked us to be a display of his good works here on earth." Lysa TerKeurst[11] (words in brackets added for clarity)

Not only was He allowing me to suffer because of Chad's sin, but some may even say He orchestrated it to be this way in my life. He thought this much of me, and of anyone else in their suffering, to allow it to happen so that His power and glory might be displayed. Don't you find this comforting like I do? None of this pain will be wasted! God is not against me, but He is always with me and for me.

Post-divorce, there would be more and more pruning. Not necessarily things that were idols either. I felt that the Lord was calling me into a season of rest. I was unsure what that looked like with three very active kids, but I did what I could to slow things down. We scaled back some of the extracurricular activities to allow for more family time together. We said "no" to some invitations to allow some margin in our evenings and weekends. We ended up being together as a family more naturally with a slower calendar, which naturally allowed for more time discipling the kids. Teaching them the things of God had tangible benefits all on its own. As I was obedient to do my part in entering into a season of rest, I was blessed over and over.

Then I got the call no one wants. More pruning. I was getting laid off from my part-time job. It wasn't much, but I sure relied on it. But praise God! I realized major expenses had already been cut the month before in the name of "rest." In the end, I could see His hand of provision getting me out of working for an unhealthy company on the brink of bankruptcy. It's in moments like this I feel like He lovingly led me back to John 15. Abide only in Him. Rely upon Him solely, not a husband or employer. While this has been a long time of pruning, I feel like it's been a way of keeping me so tightly tethered to the Father. I still have many questions from that beautiful sunset on the golf course. Did the marriage have to be pruned? Could I have fulfilled my God-given purposes without this divorce? If Chad was going to be pruned from me, why then and not earlier in the other instances of unfaithfulness? Either way, I rest in the fact that the Lord knows best and I can trust Him with my future. This pruning hasn't been punishment either, but careful, thoughtful scaling away that I would not have voluntarily done. After much reflecting and zooming out of my situation, I can truly say that my husband leaving isn't something that happened *to* me, but the good God would bring from this happened *for* me. For my good and for God's glory.

my husband leaving isn't something that happened to me, but the good God would bring from this happened for me. For my good and for God's glory.

Reflection

- Has the Lord pruned areas of your life before that didn't make sense at the time?

- What changes have come from God's pruning that you would now call a blessing?

- What idols in your life need to be cut off?

Dear Lord, thank you for being an all-knowing and loving Father. Thank you for being the best Gardener. Thank you for pruning me, even when it's so uncomfortable and turns my life upside down. I know You always have my best interests in mind and are the true source of life. I also know that You are with me and will never leave me. Help me to abide in You and bear fruit that will last. In Jesus's name, amen.

CHAPTER 5

The Already and The Not Yet

At the right time, I, the Lord, will make it happen. Isaiah 60:22 (NLT)

Waiting is not a fun process, but when you find yourself in a season of waiting, oftentimes it exponentially deepens your faith. I was a couple of months into my season when I met a new friend. She found herself walking through a marital separation, as well, not by her own choice. Her main prayer was to "wait well." I loved the sentiment, and eventually, it became my own prayer. I realized I was in a perpetual season of waiting. Waiting for the truth to come out. Waiting for a separation agreement to be made. Waiting for the divorce to be final. Waiting for my next steps to be made clear. Lord, help me wait well. I love that the Bible shows how waiting on the Lord changes us.

> *I waited patiently for the LORD; he inclined to me and heard my cry. He drew me up from the pit of destruction, out of the miry bog, and set my feet upon a rock, making my steps secure. He put a new song in my mouth, a song of praise to our God. Many will see and fear, and put their trust in the LORD. Psalms 40:1-3 (ESV)*

Waiting is a theme that is repeated over and over in the Bible. Joseph waited for nearly two decades for his wrongs to be made right. The nation of Israel waited for ages to be freed from captivity in Egypt. I've heard they waited over 400 years! Then the Israelites waited *another* forty years before they made it into the promised land. David was crowned king, but went back to tending sheep for another ten years before entering into his royal duties. But one thing was the same throughout… God was *with* them. God was *for* them. God was fighting behind the scenes for them. God was preparing them. God was setting them apart for His good works and purposes. All of these examples made their way into my quiet times and sermons I listened to throughout this season of separation from Chad. The Lord used these characters to show me what not to do during my waiting and how to wait well.

> God was with them. God was for them. God was fighting behind the scenes for them. God was preparing them.

Dr. David Jeremiah said, "God takes our setbacks and turns them into comebacks. He takes our disappointments and turns them into his appointments. And he can even take our misfortunes and turn them into a ministry. That's the grace of God."[12] Isn't that the truth? This is precisely what God does with Joseph, the Israelites, and David.

Let's take a look at the life of Joseph. Y'all buckle up because there is so much to glean from his story! When A.W. Tozer said, "It is doubtful whether God can bless a man greatly until he has hurt him deeply,"[13] this describes Joseph to a T. He was one of Jacob's youngest sons and it was a well-known fact that Joseph was Jacob's favorite son. As a teenager, he began to have incredible dreams of his future greatness. The problem was, he didn't keep quiet about these dreams and told his already jealous brothers about one of his dreams that one day they would bow down to him. To put it mildly, his brothers were less than thrilled with the idea so they conspired to kill him. They stopped short and sold Joseph off! He went to Egypt and became a slave in Potiphar's house. Joseph was a handsome guy and Potiphar's wife threw herself at him multiple times, but Joseph turned her down every time. I guess her pride took a hit, so she decided to make up a story falsely accusing him. Joseph went on to spend over ten years in jail! While he was in jail, the Lord gave him wisdom to interpret dreams. After so much waiting, he interpreted a dream for Pharoah and "was quickly brought from the dungeon" (Gen. 41:14).

In the end, Joseph was promoted to being the second-in-command over all of Egypt. This was a strategic place of authority, especially regarding the nation of Israel, particularly his brothers and the famine that would soon be plaguing them. Joseph's brothers eventually came to Egypt in search of food because they had none. Joseph was overseeing the distribution of grains and ran right into his brothers. I can only imagine

> *Joseph* **intentionally** *decided to speak kindly to the very men who betrayed him*

his surprise seeing them there. After being reunited with his brothers, he told them, *So it was God who sent me here, not you! And he is the one who made me an adviser to Pharoah—the manager of his entire palace and the governor of all Egypt* (Gen. 45:8 NLT).

He was able to see that God's hand and master plan was in all of this. The Lord used his pain and time spent waiting for good. Joseph was wise enough to realize his life and the series of misfortunes were really all a part of God's bigger plan. He didn't blame his brothers. He wasn't even bitter about what they had done to him.

As a slave, as a prisoner, and even commanding beside Pharoah, Joseph was successful and prosperous. It's said in Genesis repeatedly that "the Lord was with him." We know from the account in Genesis that Joseph was blessed by viewing his nearly twenty-year ordeal through God's perspective. When it was all said and done, Joseph told his brothers, *You intended to harm me, but God intended it for good to accomplish what is now being done, the saving of many lives* (Gen. 50:20 NIV).

Saying these words brought forgiveness and reconciliation and changed the course of history. These brothers were to be the twelve tribes of Israel! Without Joseph in the picture, they would have only been the ten tribes of Israel (Joseph had two sons who were among the twelve). It would not have been the same. But Joseph *intentionally* decided to speak kindly to the very men who betrayed him and reunited his family. I love what Christa Smith said when teaching on this interaction between Joseph and his brothers. "When you and I walk in the fullness of who we are we then release other people to walk in the fullness of who they are because we're all connected."[14] The words Joseph spoke, by God's power, set his brothers free!

Joseph was different. He was intentionally set apart for a special purpose! Joseph waited well. How can we imitate Joseph? Can we forgive and speak kindly to the people who did us wrong? Can we look for ways to be used by the Lord? How about looking for how He's setting us apart? Can we wait well in the meantime? It may look in the waiting like God is silent and not moving, but you can rest assured that when it's go-time, it will happen quickly, just as Joseph was brought *quickly* from prison.

Generations later, the Israelites grew in such size, Pharaoh came to dread them. Pharoah put slave masters over them and worked them tirelessly. They were enslaved for many generations until the Lord called Moses to set them free. Getting the Israelites out of captivity was a mission on its own, but once they were out, the nation continually sinned against God. They were bound for the promised land, but because of their sin, God would not allow them to see it. After forty years of wandering in the desert with Moses, Joshua ended up leading the nation of Israel into the promised land.

> So the Lord gave Israel all the land he had sworn to give their ancestors, and they took possession of it and settled there. The Lord gave them rest on every side, just as he had sworn to their ancestors. Not one of their enemies withstood them; the Lord gave all their enemies into their hands. Not one of all the Lord's good promises to Israel failed; every one was fulfilled. Joshua 21:43-45 (NIV)

The Israelites could have traveled directly to the promised land in less than two weeks, but there was purpose in the waiting and wandering. This is where they learned the character of God, how to honor Him, and how to fight. Bill Johnson of Bethel Church put it this way, "There are things you learn in the battle, that you need to stay in the land. There's things you learn in the fight, that build that strength of heart that enables us to live with maturity and steward well that which God has promised us."[15] Had the Israelites gone straight to the land they were promised, they would not have had the integrity or maturity it takes to stay there.

I started a new Bible Study through First 5, an app created by Proverbs 31 Ministries, just a couple of weeks before our divorce was finalized. Not surprisingly, it was titled "How to Wrestle Well When You're Worn Out in the Waiting" from the Book of Numbers. Boy, was I worn out. We should have been finalized months prior. There was setback after setback. Delay after delay. This perfectly-timed Bible study brought so many lessons and encouragement, and these daily studies continued right up until the divorce was finalized.

A few highlights I loved from this study showed the importance of giving thanks and reminded me that Jesus is with me in the wilderness. Definitely something worth noting was that grumbling and complaining was, and still is, really weighty to God. Complaining about the way things are got the Israelites pretty stiff consequences. Learning from the Israelites mistakes, instead of listing out the things not going the way we would hope, let's give thanks and praise God for what He's done. As it is right this very second, He has already done for us what we could never do on our own. If He never did anything else special for us, He's already done enough! Having a grateful heart and being thankful for what the Lord has done for us changes everything about our outlook.

> *"Here, in our hard places, Jesus walks with us in the wilderness. And one day he will walk us home to his promised land."*

Also going through the detailed history of the Israelites in Numbers 33 shows us that we can see His involvement in the life of the Israelites and how He proves His faithfulness. Finally, as First 5 author Mei Au puts it, "Here, in our hard places, Jesus walks with us in the wilderness. And one day he will walk us home to his promised land."[16] What a nugget of truth to hold onto! I know this study through the Book of Numbers was just another perfectly-timed gift from the Father to show He was with me and always would be.

After I started Numbers, my pastor spoke on "blank spaces" in the life of King David, the blank spaces being how David returned to the pasture to tend sheep *after* he'd been anointed king! I love how Pastor JD said, "Character is best formed in the blank spaces." God uses these seemingly useless times to prepare His leaders. In David's blank space, he learned humility, patience, and that God always keeps His promises. It was here that God developed David in a practical sense, too. David learned the skill with the slingshot that would come in handy when he faced Goliath. He fought a lion and a bear in this season which gave him godly confidence and courage. Here, he had plenty of time to practice playing the harp and later would become one of the world's most famous songwriters, penning most of the Psalms.

Don't waste your pasture or your suffering, be faithful in it.

Pastor JD left us with a couple takeaways that day and one stuck with me for a while. Don't despise your blank spaces. God continues to use periods of suffering to prepare us, even as adults. Don't waste your pasture or your suffering, be faithful in it.[17] "Don't waste your pasture" went up on my bathroom mirror and stayed for a couple months. But that was just the beginning of my understanding of my own pasture, my own wilderness.

The very next day after Pastor JD's sermon, I read this in the Numbers devotional plan. "The wilderness is also a place of closeness with God: an opportunity to hear Him speak, learn lessons and travel with Him on a spiritual journey. The isolation and freedom from distraction allow us to experience God more fully." -Kellye Schiffner Carver[18]

What a way to look at your period of waiting. Of course, we have the option to run to God at times like these or we can run from God. It's completely our choice. But waiting on Him, allowing Him to be your refuge, and learning more about Him on that journey is such a better use of our time. This came as such a timely reminder that He's working in this season. I was, in fact, hearing Him speak and learning all kinds of lessons.

The Lord really wanted to hammer home this point to me. It was so clear that I needed to be intentional and active in my waiting. Waiting is not just sitting around doing nothing. It's an active anticipation that God is moving. It's a quiet trusting. It's also believing that Peter said it best in 1 Peter 5:10 (NLT). *In his kindness God called you to share in his eternal glory by means of Christ Jesus. So after you have suffered a little while, he will restore, support, and strengthen you, and he will place you on a firm foundation.*

I currently receive an emailed daily devotion from my pastor. They are timely and on target with what the Lord has been trying to teach me. While I was in the midst of learning about waiting well, my pastor sent this: "If you feel like you are in a season of darkness – waiting for God to answer a prayer or bring back a child or heal up a hurt or bind up a wound–don't give up. God is up to something good and soon you will see his deliverance."[19] I think that's precisely why Paul said in his letter to the church in Rome, *But if we hope for what we do not yet have, we wait for it patiently* (Rom. 8:25 NIV).

A season of waiting is a time to draw near to the Lord, to allow Him alone to guide you while drowning out all of the noise and outside opinions. It's being still before the Lord and knowing that He is God (Ps. 46:10). And sometimes, when it's hard to be anything but frustrated, worship while you wait. Bring the sacrifice of praise. It's called a sacrifice for a reason. You won't always feel like worshiping, but sometimes that's all you can do. It changes your heart, your perspective, everything. In worship, we're so often reminded of the promises of God, which can't help but shine light on our hearts. I love the song "Your Nature" when Kari Jobe sings God's ability to make all things new, whole, and fully restored. Yes, God is more than able; our part is to believe and worship in the waiting.

> "There is no desert that Your streams can't run to
> There are no ruins that Your love won't make new
> You tell the wasteland
> That it will bloom again
> Cause it's Your nature
>
> You will restore the years that shame has stolen
> You keep the promises that You have spoken
> I know this wasteland will be whole again
> Cause it's Your nature
>
> Sing out o barren woman
> Sing out o broken man
> Stretch out your hands believing this is your promise land
> Break out of disappointment
> Break out of hopelessness
> Stretch out your hands believing this is your promise land"[20]

Don't stay in your disappointment; break out and just praise Him. Proclaiming who God is in the midst of your darkness changes everything! His light changes your heart and your perspective! Sometimes worship is your greatest weapon.

One night a few weeks after the divorce was finalized, I took my kids to worship night at our church. Sitting down in the sanctuary with our pastor praying over us, the presence of God was palpable. He was praying we would feel the Lord's presence going before us making a way, behind us, guarding us. As he prayed, I was choking up, then heard a sob. Was that me? I thought to myself, *Pull it together, Rachel.* I listened back in on Pastor JD's prayer, "that you would feel Him on both sides." Sobs again.

Not mine, but my oldest's! Ten at the time, he was overcome by the Father's presence. He was so overcome he could hardly speak, but he did eventually tell me he was so upset about who wasn't there, his dad. He missed him so bad. I just held him as we grieved together in the middle of the service. The band got up on the stage and started playing. I had the privilege of teaching him about bringing the sacrifice of praise that evening. Even for him as young as he was, it was a *sacrifice* to sing and worship when he was feeling the heartbreak so heavily. I treasured getting to witness his heart change that night as he sang about God's goodness and character. My baby was scream-singing the last song, "I'll Go Wherever," he was so hyped! He was ready to take on the world as he sang these words about the Lord working in his heart and being willing to go wherever the Lord called him.

Proclaiming who God is in the midst of your darkness changes everything!

Worship isn't just your singing and sacrificing of praise. You can be a living sacrifice. In fact we're called to, *...offer your bodies as a living sacrifice, holy and pleasing to God—this is your true and proper worship* (Rom. 12:1 NIV). Offer your time and talents to Him. It allows you to get outside of yourself and your grief. Serving inserts you into other people's lives, their pain, their struggles, and their victories. It allows you to bear each other's burdens as we're called to.

> *...offer yourselves to God as those who have been brought from death to life; and offer every part of yourself to him as an instrument of righteousness.* Romans 6:13 (NIV)

About six months into this journey, our pastor had spoken on adoption and foster care. Adoption had been on my heart for a few years already, but I was in no position to be able to make any moves on that desire. After praying about it and talking with a couple of other families in our church, my kids and I met a foster family. The husband and wife were fostering three children: a twelve-year-old special needs child, and two brothers (eighteen and nine months old) with food security issues. My kids and I started offering respite nights for the parents where we would hang out with the children. It was a small commitment, but it had a huge impact on our hearts! Huge! We celebrated every new pound the babies put on, good grades from the middle schooler, and when the youngest began to hit important milestones that he was so delayed on hitting. We cried with the family when the oldest was suddenly moved out of the foster family's home to be placed in a higher level of care. Those tears of grief helped me realize that I could love again. I could bear someone else's burdens, and it was good for my heart to do that. The same goes for my kids. The Lord stretched us to make room for these new relationships, and we are so much better for it now.

While aiming to wait well and drawing near to the Lord, cling to His promises. The Word is full of them! The week after I watched *War Room*, still so inspired by Mrs. Clara's prayer closet, I began to make small cards of Bible verses. Some verses were promises, some were reminders of the spiritual warfare we're up against, and some were on the character of God. Instead of staring at Chad's empty side of the closet, it was now filled with biblical truths. Whenever I needed encouragement or reminders of who God was, I could run to the closet and be reminded. Whenever I got ready for the day, reading these helped my heart to be ready for the battles to come being clothed in the armor of God. Some of my favorites for this season were,

- *So do not fear, for I am with you; do not be dismayed, for I am your God. I will strengthen you and help you; I will uphold you with my righteous right hand.* Isaiah 41:10 (NIV)

- *I am he who will sustain you. I have made you and I will carry you; I will sustain you and I will rescue you.* Isaiah 46:4 (NIV)

- *The weapons we fight with are not the weapons of the world. On the contrary, they have divine power to demolish strongholds.* 2 Corinthians 10:4 (NIV)

- *The Lord is a refuge for the oppressed, a stronghold in times of trouble.* Psalm 9:9 (NIV)

- *The Lord is near to all who call on him.* Psalm 145:18 (NIV)

- *He alone is my rock, my salvation* (NLT); *He is my fortress, I will never be shaken.* (NIV) Psalm 62:2

- *For our struggle is not against flesh and blood, but against the rulers, against the authorities, against the powers of this dark world and against the spiritual forces of evil in the heavenly realms.* Ephesians 6:12 (NIV)

- *Though I walk in the midst of trouble, you preserve my life. You stretch out your hand against the anger of my foes; with your right hand you will save me.* Psalm 138:7 (NIV)

- *Call to me and I will answer you and tell you great and unsearchable things you do not know.* Jeremiah 33:3 (NIV)

While waiting, you can also be still and allow the Lord to fight for you. Over and over, we have examples in the Bible where the Lord fights for the Israelites. He helps them win impossible battles. He's even made the sun stand still for an entire day to help His people win (Josh. 10:12-14)!

A couple of weeks before our divorce was finalized, there were many unknowns still left to figure out. My inner planner and go-getter were ready to start another dialogue with my soon-to-be ex-husband to finish up some last-minute items. I had every right to address the issues and I had a kind attitude about what to say, but I felt the Lord telling me to pause. He led me to Exodus 14, when the Israelites were being led away from Egypt, but were stopped by the Red Sea. The situation looked impossible and the Israelites were scared and started to protest, but Moses told them, *"Do not be afraid. Stand firm and you will see the deliverance the Lord will bring you today. The Egyptians you see today you will never see again. The Lord will fight for you; you need only to be still"* (Exod. 14:13-14 NIV).

A command and a promise. These points sank right into my heart when I needed them the most and gave specific direction to help me wait well. Be still. The Lord's got this one. I chose to listen that day and I was met with an incredible sense of peace and calm. He sustained me and ended up sorting out the very thing I was hoping to get addressed in His own timing.

Ever so timely, my pastor gave an encouraging word on how to wait. He gave four actionable steps to consider and act out while in a season of waiting:

1. **Wait patiently**–God is always good and we will see His goodness, just perhaps not in the timing we would hope for.

2. **Wait confidently**–You can be confident in God's sovereignty and that it's all in His control.

3. **Wait intimately**–What comes out when you're squeezed? We've got to be so soaked in God's promises that when we're cut, we bleed out the Spirit of God.

4. **Wait expectantly**–Think Psalm 27:14… He wants to blow our minds.[21]

These points hold so much hope and promise. These points sank right into my heart when I needed them the most and gave specific direction to help me wait well.

Reflection

- When was your last season of waiting or contending for something specific?

- When you're in a season of waiting, do you wait more like Joseph or the Israelites?

- What verse(s) from my half-empty closet are you taking with you into your next season of waiting?

Heavenly Father, thank you for this season of waiting in the wilderness. Thank you for being faithful even when I am faithless. I thank you for this season because it allows me to know You more intimately. Help me not to grow impatient in the waiting, rather help me to wait well. Thank you for the numerous examples of people who have gone before me and waited well... or not. Give me fresh eyes to see You by. May I behold You clearer than ever before. Until You give me the next assignment, help me to rest in Your sovereignty. Amen.

CHAPTER 6
My "Yes" is on the Table

continue to work out your salvation with fear and trembling, for it is God who works in you to will and to act in order to fulfill his good purpose. Phillippians 2:12-13 (NIV)

The Bible promises the blessing is on the other side of obedience. This includes being obedient even when it's counterintuitive or countercultural. There have been so many instances throughout this season when I felt like the Lord was asking me to do things. Some asks were easier than others. Some were incredibly counterintuitive and countercultural. Some asks I didn't even get to know the why or end result. Either way, I learned that you never know what all God will do because you simply obeyed.

Stay with me on this one. One of the most bristling and counter-cultural asks was that I pray for the restoration of our marriage. I knew Chad had been unfaithful multiple times and had yet to be honest with me about them. I was vehemently opposed to seeing the marriage restored. I had to pray that the Lord would change my mind about things, too. This was all leading up to our fifteenth anniversary. I prayed this way for about three weeks. I wrote a letter, writing out the wedding vows we had promised to each other. I quoted Isaiah

the blessing is on the other side of obedience.

54:10 (NIV) so he would, again, be reminded of the Savior's love for him among other things and gave it to him! *"Though the mountains be shaken and the hills be removed, yet my unfailing love for you will not be shaken nor my covenant of peace be removed," says the Lord, who has compassion on you.* I still can't believe it went that far. I found out more instances of Chad being unfaithful during our marriage just days after I gave him the note. I immediately knew I was released from praying that way, but why? Why was I convicted to pray that way in the first place?!

It was undeniably a faith-builder for me. I was stepping out on a very unsettled sea to pray that way. It was grossly uncomfortable. It was refining. All I know is God promises His Word does not return void, but achieves the purpose it was sent for. It cannot be a negative thing that Chad was reminded of God's great and unfailing love for him.

In the state where I live, a couple must be separated for one year to be eligible to file for divorce. Before filing, a separation agreement needed to be in place. By and large, there was no progress made toward a mutual agreement over the first eleven months apart. I knew mediation was coming to help us determine how things would be split, but I had reached such an apathetic place. One of the major sticking points was housing. Chad was really pushing for us to sell the house so we could realize the profits from the current housing boom. I was hoping not to have any further disruption for the kids by having to move, but it had worn on for so long that I didn't care where the kids and I would live long-term… until the Lord spoke to me about it.

Just before the one-year mark, I attended a women's conference. I knew without a shadow of a doubt that one of the messages was directed at me, giving me specific direction for going forward. I heard the Holy Spirit commissioning me to "stay and fight" for the home we were in. It was the house we had bought together a few months before he walked out. Once I fully understood how I was to go about this, I went to work. I gave my offer, similar to the widow in 1 Kings 17. When Elijah came to a pagan widowed, single mother asking her to make him bread so that he could eat, the widow didn't believe that was possible. She didn't have much, just a little oil and flour, and didn't see it working out, let alone being able to make a loaf of bread… but God. He stepped in. He provided. The widow and her family ate and were sustained. Not only that, but her oil and flour never ran out just as Elijah promised her. I watched over the next few weeks as the Lord took my proverbial oil and flour and worked everything out just as He gave me the faith to believe He would. After a long, heart-wrenching day of meditating, I got to tell the children that we were staying in the house! I watched as I offered up what I had in obedience and pure faith turn into a miracle and a major blessing.

abiding is "a seamless connection to the heart of God."

Jesus modeled for us what it is to obey and the miracle, or the blessing, that comes from obedience. Hebrews 5:7-9 (NIV) tells us,

> *During the days of Jesus' life on earth, he offered up prayers and petitions with fervent cries and tears to the one who could save him from death, and he was heard because of his reverent submission. Son though he was, he learned obedience from what he suffered and, once made perfect, he became the source of eternal salvation for all who obey him.*

His flesh didn't want to die the awful death of a crucifixion, but in the end, He did because He knew what it meant for us. We have life and salvation from His ultimate act of obedience.

Step out. Take a risk. Do that hard thing God is asking of you. What do you really stand to lose?

Abiding is a connection to the Lord when we rest in revering Him for all He is while knowing He has our best interests at heart. Bill Johnson put it simply that abiding is "a seamless connection to the heart of God."[22] Abiding is the basis of our relationship with Christ. It's our reading and *knowing* of the Word, the awareness of the presence of God, our time spent in prayer, worshiping and listening for the voice of God, and our communing with other believers. Abiding is trusting in God and in His promises.

I learned so much about the word "abide" this year. As I mentioned earlier, it was my word for the year when Chad left us. That was no accident. The reminder of "abide in me and I in you" was the very first thing I saw after the words left my husband's lips. Chad might be leaving, but God never would. Now, more than ever, I would need to learn what it means to abide. More than anything else, it's a posture of the heart in full surrender to Jesus. It's a calm and peace you have when your situation dictates that you shouldn't. I love the song "Firm Foundation (He Won't)" and how it speaks to the posture of abiding.

> "I've still got joy in chaos
> I've got peace that makes no sense
> I won't be going under
> I'm not held by my own strength
> 'Cause I've built my life on Jesus
> He's never let me down
> He's faithful through every season
> So why would He fail now?
> He won't"[23]

Over the years and during this season specifically, the Lord has proven Himself over and over. He's capable of providing a way out and/or through every situation I've faced. For me, abiding is preaching to myself the goodness of God when I'm tempted to dive into despair over whatever I'm faced with. It's reminding myself of how He has provided or sustained me so far and asking myself why He would fail now. It doesn't make sense that He would stop or leave me now. Just like any other posture your heart make take shape in, it is a conscious choice to abide in Christ.

As a part of the agreement to keep the house, I needed to get Chad's name off of everything. The problem was, to keep up with the sudden, post-COVID boom in real estate, the mortgage rates were skyrocketing. When we purchased the house, rates were at an historic low. I would not be able to afford a payment on the new rates, but I knew God had called me to stay and fight for us to stay there, so why wouldn't He make a way? I refused to let my mind worry about it. I trusted and rested in Him. Following the Lord's prompts, I made a few phone calls. I watched the Lord work everything out. It worked in a way I never saw coming, but isn't that just how He works? This showed me, again, that obedience, coupled with abiding in Christ, is a recipe for a miracle.

My kids were His before they were mine and I can rest knowing Jesus will always have their best interests at heart.

Obedience and abiding in Christ is just as important as it relates to being a single mom and doing this parenting gig solo. When there is no one else to shoulder the hurtful things the kids might say to you or the blatant disrespect, when no one else can step in, when you're too tired and weary to say another word, it's time to lean into the Lord and see what He has for you. My kids were His before they were mine and I can rest knowing Jesus will always have their best interests at heart. Even though it's hard to believe, He actually loves them more than I ever could. I love to go back and think about the children's dedication at church. It was then I was reminded the kids are only mine for a short while and to be intentional, making the most of every opportunity. This idea is even more important when I'm the kids' main disciplinarian, source of guidance, and teacher of God's Word.

Throughout this season of separation and single parenting, I've learned I'm not really alone in this. Having a head knowledge of the Lord always being present and actually experiencing His nearness in times of need is something entirely different. When you call on Him in your situation, His Spirit *will* faithfully guide you. A girlfriend in my small group introduced me to a new process I've found wisdom in and witnessed some pretty amazing outcomes because of it. The idea was: when you're at the end of your rope and don't know how to handle a situation or the proper avenue of discipline, take a step back and consult with the children's heavenly Father. Without throwing the kids' father under the bus and just calling things for what they were, the kids agreed and understood. Their father was not physically present nor was he emotionally available to help co-parent when it was time to discipline, and my kids and I knew it would be pointless to try to reach out. However, the kids know they have a heavenly Father who will never leave them nor forsake them and loves them without fail. So, in those tough moments of not knowing what to do, I would let them know that I was going to take a step back and ask their heavenly Father what to do. Sometimes, it would be pretty quick that I felt led to move in a certain direction, while other times it took days. Regardless, the Lord has been faithful every single time I've invited Him into my single parenting.

> *Operating out of grace and kindness is exactly how the Lord deals with us, so it made perfect sense to try to do that with the person who hurt me the most*

I've embraced the verse, *All your children shall be taught by the Lord, and great shall be the peace of your children* (Isa. 54:13 ESV). I believe this is happening every time I petition the Lord to be a part of this parenting journey. If I'm being led by His Spirit, He's the actual one teaching the children. Sometimes, He'll lead me to apologize to the kids for whatever I've done wrong before I do anything else. There's that element of humbling obedience again! Sometimes He'll give me wisdom about something that is happening in the spiritual realm that sheds light on the situation and other times He'll lead me into what to do. It's so easy to lash out and exact an ungodly punishment you think they deserve, and the Lord knows I'm guilty of doing just that, but doesn't that just make the Enemy of our souls so happy when we do? Satan wants to create rifts within the home and see resentment and bitterness abound. I find so much more peace and resolve when I seek the Lord first. It is possible, by His grace, to abide in Him even in single parenting, and I believe this is how we can rest in Him.

Another space where I feel the Lord has called me to be faithfully obedient is in my communication with Chad. Once things were close to being settled, I felt the Lord press me in that all of my communication with him should be full of grace and kindness. This is where walking out forgiveness became even more real. This went against every fiber of my being, especially when he was verbally attacking me, but ultimately, what could my words do to bring about justice? Sure, saying nasty things may make me feel better for a moment, but it bred further dysfunction and proved to be fruitless. Most importantly, I had to ask myself what kind of message I was sending if I spoke nastily. Operating out of grace and kindness is exactly how the Lord deals with us, so it made perfect sense to try to do that with the person who hurt me the most, even if that meant apologizing to Chad when I fell short. Kindness leads to repentance after all.

I've learned through all of these experiences that obedience is most powerful when we don't know the end result. We may not have a clue why or where we're being led, or we might know and not want to go there. Whatever the case is, I pray you feel emboldened to put your "yes" on the table.

Reflection

- Have you ever struggled with doing something you felt like the Lord was asking of you?

- Looking back, how have you tried to do things in your own strength, in turn, not abiding in Christ?

- Going forward, what can you do differently to make sure you're obedient and abiding in the Lord?

> *Dear Jesus, thank you for being the ultimate example of obedience. Thank you for Your Word and Spirit that guides me into all truth and show me how to honor You in every aspect of my life. Teach me to abide in You and have a heart bent toward obedience to You. Give me the courage to obey You even when it's countercultural. Forgive me when I fall desperately short of the mark. Amen.*

CHAPTER 7
I Will Not Be Silent

We're told in Scripture over and over that our battle is not against flesh and blood. There is an Enemy of our souls who does not want anyone to come to salvation, and he prowls around like a roaring lion seeking for someone to devour (1 Pet. 5:8). He is so crafty and devious and loves to fly under the radar, but Satan is real, and I've seen the upheaval and spiritual attacks throughout this season.

It would be so easy for me to place blame solely on Chad and his mistress for the upheaval of our family. The fact of the matter is that while we are living our lives, there is a simultaneous world going on that greatly impacts our everyday experiences. One minute we can have our eyes fixed on Jesus, the next there's a huge temptation lurking around the corner. If we're not secure enough in our identity in the Lord, it's so easy to succumb to the temptations of this world. If we know the Enemy is constantly on the prowl, we can also know he will try to trip us up repeatedly to see what eventually makes us fall. Once the first step of disobedience is taken against the Lord, it gets easy and effortless to continue walking in disobedience. Before you know it, you're running so fast in the other direction. You can't even hear the tiniest whisper of conviction. This

> the spiritual realm is always happening, whether we believe it or not, but in Christ, we already have the victory.

indifference is right where the Enemy would like to see all of us, under his thumb and not caring about the consequences.

Once I could zoom out and see that was exactly where Chad was, and believe me it took time to care, I could have compassion for him. He was running so fast into a life of deceit and catering to self without considering the consequences. He was firmly in the grip of the Enemy of our soul. His heart was hardened, and he had little regard for how his actions would affect his family.

Now, get this. While it does say the Enemy prowls around seeking someone to devour, it doesn't say he *may* devour whoever he wants. In Christ, we are given the authority to take a stand and have victory over the Enemy. We can choose to walk in our God-given inheritance as a co-heir with Christ or succumb to the temptations and pressures presented so enticingly before us.

The Lord has really opened my eyes to the spiritual side of things since Chad left the family. I've seen it in his life, attacks against myself, and even attacks directed at my kids. Sometimes, the attacks were clear as day. Other times, it was more of a hunch. The fact is, the spiritual realm is *always happening*, whether we believe it or not, but in Christ, we already have the victory.

> *For though we live in the world, we do not wage war as the world does. The weapons we fight with are not the weapons of the world. On the contrary, they have divine power to demolish strongholds.* 2 Corinthians 10:3-4 (NIV)

A couple months in, the Lord had already been working on my heart. I recognized I had wrongly idolized Chad and our marriage. My heart was already softening to forgive the man who hurt me deeply. I began speaking to friends and family about God's goodness in my awful situation. The Enemy was angry and wanted me to stay quiet.

One night, I awoke suddenly to the distinct sound of clapping in my hallway. It was 3 a.m., and I saw an ugly black figure standing next to my bed. I instantly knew it wasn't good in my spirit. As it reached toward my neck, I felt it would rip out my vocal cords or strangle me to death. I immediately sensed it was on a mission to scare me into complete silence. I could barely speak as I started trying to pray. "Jesus!" was all I could squeak out. The thing shrunk back, but was still present.

I sat up and flipped on the light. Oddly, it was freezing in my room. I'm a Florida girl, but I don't keep it frigid in my house. This was bone-chilling cold; way colder than what the AC was set to. I reached for my phone, but couldn't get the screen to light up so that I could make a call. I told Alexa to turn on worship music so the atmosphere would be peaceful and usher in the presence of God; it wouldn't respond to my several attempts. I saw the blue light appear on the Alexa, so I knew it had heard me, but would not comply with my requests. I finally got the phone to turn on so I could call my mom or any other spiritual warrior I could think of. "All circuits are busy. Your call could not go through," the automated voice responded. *What was happening*?! I was shaking and crying by that time.

While trying to make calls and get warm, something shifted in my heart. I was convicted of sin and became humble before the Lord and repentant. I was finally able to say out loud, "Jesus, be near. Satan, I rebuke you in Jesus's name. You have to leave." It was gone immediately.

I made seven calls before I could get any of them to ring, let alone anyone answer. I'm sure I sounded completely out of my mind, but my mom has seen a lot in her time. I put her on speaker and we prayed together over the situation and my house. I sat right in the spot I had heard the clapping come from. The veil between heaven and earth got especially thin in that moment. I knew the attack was over and the Holy Spirit was there with me. I would not be scared into silence. This just gave me a stronger conviction to share my testimony. God would get the glory from this awful situation. I slept like a baby that night, falling asleep to the words of "Whole Heart" again:

> "That I might stand
> With more reasons to sing than to fear

You pulled me from the clay
Set me on a rock
Called me by Your Name
And made my heart whole again"[24]

Many were joining me in prayer for discernment about the reason behind the attack. A couple days later, I found out from the other woman's husband that Chad had broken things off with his mistress just a few hours prior to the attack. This seemed to confirm my sense that the Enemy was angry. Was Chad's heart softening to the Holy Spirit's convictions? Was their breakup the driving factor behind my attack?

Certainly up until that moment, sleep had been a challenge after Chad's leaving. For the next couple of months, I would wake up around 3 a.m. like clockwork, but they were different scenarios entirely. It was more of a sweet communion with God in the middle of the night. I would go into my closet where I had pinned up all of those verses. I would read the verses and pray a few back to God, asking to see those promises come to life in my scenario, my family's, or my friends'. It would all depend on who He placed on my heart that night.

so much is left on the table, like miracles and breakthroughs, simply because we do not ask.

One night while praying, I had the revelation that weeks before the attack happened, my support network had started praying fervently for Chad's relationship with this woman to be broken up. That relationship represented a stronghold and claiming 2 Corinthians 10:4 over that relationship, God did just that. He demolished that stronghold in Chad's life.

God doesn't need His children to remind Him of the things in His Word; it is His Word, after all. But it's such a faith builder to personally ask for the promises and then see them come to life. Would they have happened anyway? They say so much is left on the table, like miracles and breakthroughs, simply because we do not ask. So, ask away! Pray that His will is done.

> *Ask and it will be given to you; seek and you will find; knock and the door will be opened to you. For everyone who asks receives; the one who seeks finds; and to the one who knocks, the door will be opened.* Matthew 7:7-8 (NIV)

Later on, I'd begun noticing some pretty outrageous and uncharacteristic behavior from the kids once they would come home from a weekend at their dad's house. I know the back and forth is hard on any child, but I felt like there was more to it and began thinking about the spiritual aspect of the situation. Of course, I would pray over the children when they went to their dad's house, but I knew I needed to pray more earnestly and specifically. It all came to light one day in the grocery store. I had all three kids and one in particular was acting out big time. I remember he made such a scene in the deli, yelling atrocious things about the options for lunch that day. I bluntly asked what was wrong with him. He angrily told me he didn't know. I gave up on figuring out lunch in the deli. We started shopping again and in the bread aisle, my son blurted out, "I don't know why, Mom, but I feel like I'm cursed every time I come home from Dad's house."

In an instant, I had chills down my spine and knew nothing else mattered at that moment. We immediately stopped right there in the bread aisle and prayed out loud, rebuking whatever Satan was up to and trying to accomplish. Under my hands, I could feel my son instantly drop his shoulders as his body began to relax. I knew we'd nailed it. He didn't say much more in the store that day other than, "I'm glad you prayed. I feel so much better." My precious baby.

"Why has the attack been so strong? If you were not carrying Jesus, if you were not sent for a purpose, if there was not a prophecy over your life, you wouldn't be feeling any pain. The pain is a labor pain. You're about to bring something forth." -Steven Furtick[25]

I believe it's part of our duties as Christians to be aware of what's going on in the spiritual kingdom. Some are more gifted in this than others, but the Spirit is faithful to give wisdom and discernment when asked. The Enemy is real and very active in the life of believers, even when we're in the midst of the heaviest grief we've ever known. Perhaps Satan is even more active in our grief because we're so vulnerable, but we have to be alert to call it what it is. Paul spelled it out for us in his letter to the church at Ephesus.

> *Finally, be strong in the Lord and in his mighty power. Put on the full armor of God, so that you can take your stand against the devil's schemes. For our struggle is not against flesh and blood, but against the rulers, against the authorities, against the powers of this dark world and against the spiritual forces of evil in the heavenly realms. Therefore put on the full armor of God, so that when the day of evil comes, you may be able to stand your ground, and after you have done everything, to stand. Stand firm then, with the belt of truth buckled around your waist, with the breastplate of righteousness in place, and with your feet fitted with the readiness that comes from the gospel of peace. In addition to all this, take up the shield of faith, with which you can extinguish all the flaming arrows of the evil one. Take the helmet of salvation and the sword of the Spirit, which is the word of God.* Ephesians 6:10-17 (NIV)

I know this is a big passage and there is a lot to dissect. Paul is letting us know there are *many* things in a Christian's toolbox to defend ourselves against the Enemy's tactics, the armor of God. Paul was very familiar with a Roman soldier's garb having spent time in prison, so many of these pieces of the armor overlap. Here's a very basic example of what these different pieces are:

- The **belt of truth** is the most important piece because without it, most of the armor could not stay on. It holstered the sword and the breastplate was fasted to it. In Paul's day, the Roman soldier's belt was much thicker and heavier than a belt we would wear now. Simply put, it is truth. Truth is meant to guide our every word, thought, and action.

- The **breastplate of righteousness** requires our obedience or walking rightly with God. Yes, our own righteousness is as filthy rags, but by accepting the gift of salvation and walking by the Spirit, we are able to put on Christ's righteousness as our own.

- The **shoes of the gospel of peace** give us an image we know is only from the Lord. Shoes protect our feet and help us stand firm, just as peace does to our hearts. Peace is a fruit of the Spirit and the gospel is the good news of Jesus. Knowing Him and finding our identity in Him gives us peace that surpasses all understanding.

- The **shield of faith** protects us from attacks and fiery arrows of the Enemy. Think of it as a blanket of protection. It's large and can be used both defensively and offensively. When we're fighting the Enemy, sometimes we have to go on the offensive and that requires our bold, unwavering faith.

- The **helmet of salvation** speaks to our hearts receiving salvation and continuing to work that out through sanctification. The helmet also protects our thought life. What we think about and dwell on matters and should be lined up against the truth. Having our minds renewed is crucial. As I have heard it said, you become what you behold.

- Lastly, the **sword of the Spirit** which is the Word of God. Knowing the Bible allows properly fighting off the Enemy, as Jesus modeled when He was tempted in the wilderness (Luke 4:1-13). Jesus recognized the devil's attempts at tempting Him by twisting the Word, in turn, Jesus recited verses to speak truth every time.

Get this. Do you see how the armor only covers the front? Bill Johnson pointed out in a sermon, "There was no armor on their back because never does the believer turn and run. The believer is fighting from the victory of Christ, towards an expressed victory in the earth. We're not fighting for the defeat of the enemy. He's already been defeated."[26]

Bottom line, we have to remember who we're fighting against. It's not the nasty family member or hurtful friend. Look over their shoulder, so to speak. We must know we are children of the King who is always *with* us and that the blood He sacrificed on our behalf has supernatural power! Surrendering, finding refuge, and abiding in Christ is critical. When we're in crisis or heavy grief, sometimes that's all we can do. Guess what? When you call on Him, He promises to protect and deliver you. Every. Single. Time.

Surrendering, finding refuge, and abiding in Christ is critical.

If you say, "The Lord is my refuge," and you make the Most High your dwelling, no harm will overtake you, no disaster will come near your tent. For he will command his angels concerning you to guard you in all your ways; they will lift you up in their hands, so that you will not strike your foot against a stone. You will tread on the lion and the cobra; you will trample the great lion and the serpent. "Because he loves me," says the Lord, "I will rescue him; I will protect him, for he acknowledges my name. He will call on me, and I will answer him; I will be with him in trouble, I will deliver him and honor him. With long life I will satisfy him and show him my salvation." Psalms 91:9-16 (NIV)

"So let's answer the question why am I facing attack? Because Jesus loves you, and the enemy hates you. Though God's promises and plans will ultimately prevail, the devil will stop at nothing to distract, discourage or derail you from your high calling in Jesus Christ." -Susie Larson[27]

Friend, stand firm in Him and stay the course.

Reflection

- Have you ever felt powerless to the schemes of the Enemy?

- What significance does the spiritual realm have on your personal faith walk?

- How can you walk forward confidently in your God-given authority because of the finished work of the cross?

Dear Jesus, thank you for the power that is in Your precious blood! Sometimes the knowledge of what You've done and being called Your child is just too much to comprehend. I love that I can draw on that power to fight against the schemes of the Enemy. I pray that You would open my eyes to the things of darkness happening around me. I pray that You would give me courage to immediately address the issues with tenacity. Lord, be a shield about me! Thank you for the victory in advance! May I be careful to give You the glory. Amen

CHAPTER 8

Does Jesus Really Know How I Feel?

"The question remains, is God paying attention? If so, why doesn't he do something? I say he has, he did, he is doing something, and he will do something.

"The subjects can only be approached by the cross. That old, rugged cross so despised by the world. The very worst thing that has ever happened in human history turns out to be the very best thing because it saves me. It saves the world. And so God's love, which was represented, demonstrated to us in His giving His son Jesus to die on the cross, has been brought together in harmony with suffering.

"You see, this is the crux of the question. And those of you have studied Latin may remember that the word crux is the Latin word, crux for cross. It's only in the cross that we can begin to harmonize the seeming contradiction between suffering and love. And we will never understand suffering unless we understand the love of God."
-Elisabeth Elliot[28]

I was craving to be comforted. People would send their well-wishes and well-meaning Bible verses. They tried their best, but where I felt the most comfort was in knowing that Jesus understood my pain. Intimately. Isaiah said He is a man of sorrows and is acquainted with our grief (Isa. 53:3), but is He really? Does Jesus *really* know how I feel? I asked myself exactly that, doubtful in my own grief until I did my research to remind myself of the timeless truth.

Jesus felt soul crushing pain. Jesus was betrayed and felt abandoned. He was humiliated and heartbroken. Yes, He was fully God, but fully man. He would bleed the very same way we do when He got cut. Likewise, He felt the same emotions we do. And if He felt every emotion we do, then no emotion in and of itself can be a sin as He was a sinless man. Of course, what matters is what you do with those emotions and how you act them out. The Bible lays out clear examples of how and when Jesus felt these things.

Jesus Felt Soul Crushing Pain

Jesus knew the discipline of getting away from the chaos of the world to get alone with the Father. He modeled for us what it is to press into the "secret place." He knew what was coming, gathered a couple friends and went to pray.

> *He took Peter and Zebedee's two sons, James and John, and he became anguished and distressed. He told them, "My soul is crushed with grief to the point of death. Stay here and keep watch with me." He went on a little farther and bowed with his face to the ground, praying, "My Father! If it is possible, let this cup of suffering be taken away from me. Yet I want your will to be done, not mine."* Matthew 26:37-39 (NLT)

In Mark 14:32-34 (MSG), it says, *He sank into a pit of suffocating darkness. He told them, "I feel bad enough right now to die."* His heart was so consumed by grief He said He felt like He was dying. He was crying out to God for the suffering to not happen. Doesn't that sound familiar?

> *And being in agony he prayed more earnestly; and his sweat became like great drops of blood falling down to the ground.* Luke 22:44 (ESV)

Yeah, He gets it. Your body is so undone by sorrow it acts in ways that are extremely outside of the norm. While in this garden, sweating blood, He begged and pleaded with the Father not to let this happen. But then, only as someone who truly loves the Father could, He prayed that the Lord's will would be done, not His.

He was Betrayed by One of His Best Friends, Judas

> *And as they were eating, he said, "Truly, I say to you, one of you will betray me." He answered, "He who has dipped his hand in the dish with me will betray me. The Son of Man goes as it is written of him, but woe to that man by whom the Son of Man is betrayed! It would have been better for that man if he had not been born." Judas, who would betray him, answered, "Is it I, Rabbi?" He said to him, "You have said so."* Matthew 26:21, 23-25 (ESV)

Of course, being fully God, Jesus knew the future, but that doesn't mean the betrayal didn't hurt. Shortly after this conversation with Judas, He escaped to the garden with a couple of his close friends to go pray, knowing full well that He was about to be betrayed which would eventually lead to his death. Praying earnestly, He felt that soul crushing pain. In comes Judas, with a large group of armed men, ready to arrest Jesus.

being fully God, Jesus knew the future, but that doesn't mean the betrayal didn't hurt.

> *Now the betrayer had given them a sign, saying, "The one I will kiss is the man; seize him." And he came up to Jesus at once and said, "Greetings, Rabbi!" And he kissed him. Jesus said to him, "Friend, do what you came to do." Then they came up and laid hands on Jesus and seized him.* Matthew 26:48-50 (ESV)

I can only imagine what He must have felt right then being betrayed by one of His closest friends, especially considering the depths and consequences of this betrayal. While the betrayal I experienced didn't mean my death, it brings me comfort to know He's familiar with my pain.

Jesus Was Humiliated

After He was arrested and brought before the chief priest for sentencing, Jesus was said to be guilty...

> *Then they spit in his face and struck him with their fists. Others slapped him.* Matthew 26:67 (NIV)

Pilate ordered Jesus to be beaten and then crucified. But that wasn't enough, the humiliation continued.

> *They stripped him and put a scarlet robe on him. They wove thorn branches into a crown and put it on his head, and they placed a reed stick in his right hand as a scepter. Then they knelt before him in mockery and taunted, "Hail! King of the Jews!" And they spit on him and grabbed the stick and struck him on the head with it.* Matthew 27:28-30 (NLT)

Reading this breaks my heart. His pain was so much greater than anything I have ever experienced, and yet He still cares that I found myself in a heartbroken, soul crushing space.

Jesus Was Abandoned

As He hung on the cross, Jesus bore our sins, every single one of them. Sins from our youth, our present, and sins we haven't even committed yet. He, a holy, sinless man, took on the sins of the world.

> *At noon, darkness fell across the whole land until three o'clock. At about three o'clock, Jesus called out with a loud voice, "Eli, Eli, lema sabachthani?" which means "My God, my God, why have you abandoned me?"* Matthew 27:45-46 (NLT)

I'm no Bible scholar, but they talk about that darkness as it relates to our sins Jesus took on in that moment. God, the Father, couldn't look at His Son anymore covered in the sins of the world. Jesus must have felt so alone. All the while, He continued to be mocked and humiliated by the bystanders.

I can definitely see how what Isaiah said in Chapter 53 was no exaggeration.

> *He was despised and rejected—a man of sorrows, acquainted with deepest grief. We turned out backs on him and looked the other way. He was despised, and we did not care. Yet it was our weaknesses he carried; it was our sorrows that weighed him down. And we thought his troubles were a punishment from God, a punishment for his own sins! But he was pierced for our rebellion, crushed for our sins. He was beaten so we could be whole. He was whipped so we could be healed.* Isaiah 53:4-5 (NLT)

His pain was so much greater than anything I have ever experienced, and yet He still cares that I found myself in a heartbroken, soul crushing space.

Then there's the synopsis in Hebrews of what Jesus did along with a charge to Christ followers.

> *Keep your eyes on Jesus, who both began and finished this race we're in. Study how he did it. Because he never lost sight of where he was headed—that exhilarating finish in and with God—he could put up with anything along the way: Cross, shame, whatever. And now he's there, in the place of honor, right alongside God.* Hebrews 12:2 (MSG)

Yes. He did all of that for us. For you. For me. For our kids and grand-kids. Even for that person who hurt you the most. He is our Redeemer. He is our Savior. He is our Hope. He wants you just as you are. You are loved. You are chosen. You are His! This is the good news. Jesus, perfect as He was, endured all of this and more. He was crucified, defeated hell, and rose from the dead on the third day! This is why we have the hope of heaven. Jesus has already won the victory.

Have you made the decision to believe in Him and what He's done for you? If you haven't yet, here's your cordial invitation to your seat at the table. There is room for you, even with your grief and messes. He gets it and He cares. Resting in Him, you *will* be made whole again. I promise He will gently gather up the pieces of your shattered heart, or proverbial jar, and hold you together as only He can. He will lift the sadness and be your joy!

"Oh, the perfect Son of God
In all His innocence
Here walking in the dirt with you and me
He knows what living is
He's acquainted with our grief
Man of sorrows, Son of suffering
The blood and tears
How can it be?
There's a God who weeps

There's a God who bleeds
Oh, praise the One
Who would reach for me
Hallelujah to the Son of suffering"
-Bethel Worship[29]

Reflection

- Have you felt alone in your suffering?

- How does Jesus's death on the cross humble you?

- What parts of your story are infused with comfort and hope because of Jesus's experience with betrayal and abandonment, but ultimately because of His resurrection?

Oh, Lord, what an incredible sacrifice You made for me! I believe You lived a blameless life, bled, died in my place, and were raised to life on the third day. I believe You are God's perfect Lamb. Please forgive me of all of my sins and make my heart clean. I want to walk with You every day for the rest of my life. I find great comfort in knowing You know my heart's pain intimately. Help me to rest in You.

Friend, if you prayed that prayer for the first time, I encourage you to reach out to someone you know who loves the Lord. Tell someone! Don't keep this to yourself.

CHAPTER 9

The Arms That Hold Me Now

The Lord is my shepherd; I have what I need. He lets me lie down in green pastures; he leads me beside quiet waters. He renews my life; he leads me along the right paths for his name's sake. Even when I go through the darkest valley, I fear no danger, for you are with me; your rod and your staff— they comfort me. You prepare a table before me in the presence of my enemies; you anoint my head with oil; my cup overflows. Only goodness and faithful love will pursue me all the days of my life, and I will dwell in the house of the Lord as long as I live. Psalms 23:1-6 (CSB)

Psalm 23 gives us a beautiful image of someone who has chosen to trust God. They've decided to view God as their Shepherd. They know His goodness and love, or "hesed," will always follow them. Sheep depend on their shepherd for everything- food, safety, and health. Placing our broken lives in God's hands is an act of trust.

It's funny. I realize this is another piece of scripture the Lord kept hitting me with over and over during this season. My pastor spoke on it for several weeks, my small group read Philip Keller's book *A Shepherd Looks at Psalm 23*, and it was even in a few of the devotions I read all in the same time frame. The Lord really wanted me to understand that because He is my Shepherd, I have no needs. He walks with me in the dark and sad places. I'm not alone. He is in control and I can trust Him.

His goodness and mercy will always chase me down. Philip Keller said, "There are still valleys to walk through during our remaining days. These need not be 'dead end' streets. The disappointments, the frustrations, the discouragements, the dilemmas, the dark, difficult days, though they be shadowed valleys, need not be disasters. They can be the road to higher ground in our walk with God."[30]

> *Placing our broken lives in God's hands is an act of trust.*

The week my pastor spoke on "I Have No Needs," I took notes in a frenzy. The message was saturated in wisdom. Comparing Psalm 23 to the life of Job, he found three types of faith:

1. **The faith of prosperity**–Here you get all of the blessings of God… until it all falls apart.

2. **The faith of desperation**–Even though it's all falling apart, your heart is postured to trust Him. *Though He slay me, yet will I trust Him* (Job 13:15 NKJV).

3. **The faith of sufficiency**–This is a faith that rejoices, sits silently and is calm in the presence of the Shepherd. Job went from believing the goodness of God to *feeling* it. More than just trusting, Job *knew* that his Redeemer was alive and stood with him.[31]

Elisabeth Elliot says it plainly in her book *Suffering is Never for Nothing*, "I am either held in the Everlasting Arms or I'm at the mercy of chance and I have to trust Him or deny Him."[32] Just like anything else in this life, we have a choice here.

There have been countless times throughout the last couple of years God has made it unequivocally clear that He went before me, that He knew this was coming. All of these little revelations make me trust Him more and more.

I'm one who marks up the pages of my Bible, be it sermon notes, quotes, or little revelations. I don't always date the notes, but sometimes I do. Once I found myself in this treacherous season, I dove into the Word more than ever. I found myself in Exodus 16 where the Lord sustains the Israelites with the gift of manna every day. Without fail, He provided what they needed every morning. I wrote a note, "*Provision = He only gave them enough for each day at a time.*" This particular note was dated three years exactly to the day before Chad walked out on us. I know this was far from a coincidence, but a perfectly timed word from God that He knew I would need in a couple years. A sweet reminder that He went before us, He alone is Jehovah Jireh and would provide for all of our needs. I have seen Him provide just enough for each of our days faithfully. He is a Man of His Word. How can we not trust Him? Bonus! When we chose to trust Him, He promises to keep us in perfect peace (Isa. 26:3)!

Trust is such a substantial word. It's a heavy concept at any given time, but especially when your heart is shattered and trying to believe anyone has good in them. Trust, as it relates to a Christian, looks like faith. We walk by faith and not by sight. God being found trustworthy for His children looks like Him being faithful. Faithful to do what He said He would do, faithful to His promises, faithful to the Word He spoke over you.

God has a pretty perfect track record for being faithful. Can you look back over your life and see God's hand? Did He provide in some amazing ways that you never saw coming? Did He close the door on a situation you may not have wanted, but looking back now you can see it was for your good? Did He heal that wound a family member left years ago? Looking back at all of the ways the Lord has had His hand in our lives, it becomes easier to recognize when He's on the move. It also makes it easier to trust and have faith, believing He can do it all over again. Whenever I'm tempted to act on my own because I don't see the Lord working fast enough, this verse brings me pause and promise.

> *Yet the Lord longs to be gracious to you; therefore he will rise up to show you compassion. For the Lord is a God of justice. Blessed are all who wait for him!* Isaiah 30:18 (NIV)

Having faith doesn't stop bad things from happening to us. Having faith and living for God, doesn't mean happily ever after. On the contrary, we live in a fallen world and Satan keeps coming for you. The Enemy would much rather see you discouraged and doubtful about who God is. Having faith keeps His faithfulness at the forefront. It remembers what He's done and promised to do. When someone trusts the Lord with their life, they stop striving to control everything on their own. They respond in faith and find the peace and rest that God alone offers.

> *So do not throw away this confident trust in the Lord. Remember the great reward it brings you! Patient endurance is what you need now, so that you will continue to do God's will. Then you will receive all that he has promised.* Hebrews 10:35-36 (NLT)

When I think about trusting God, I go back to this story over and over, so I think it bears repeating. I was a freshman in college six months prior to meeting Chad, and the Lord led me to Isaiah 54 one night in my dorm room. He impressed on my heart that it was a word for me.

> *[1]"Sing, barren woman, you who never bore a child; burst into song, shout for joy, you who were never in labor; because more are the children of the desolate woman than of her who has a husband," says the Lord. [2]"Enlarge the*

place of your tent, stretch your tent curtains wide, do not hold back; lengthen your cords, strengthen your stakes. ³For you will spread out to the right and to the left; your descendants will dispossess nations and settle in their desolate cities. ⁴"Do not be afraid; you will not be put to shame. Do not fear disgrace; you will not be humiliated. You will forget the shame of your youth and remember no more the reproach of your widowhood. ⁵For your Maker is your husband— the Lord Almighty is his name— the Holy One of Israel is your Redeemer; he is called the God of all the earth. ⁶The Lord will call you back as if you were a wife deserted and distressed in spirit— a wife who married young, only to be rejected," says your God. ⁷"For a brief moment I abandoned you, but with deep compassion I will bring you back. ⁸In a surge of anger I hid my face from you for a moment, but with everlasting kindness I will have compassion on you," says the Lord your Redeemer. ⁹"To me this is like the days of Noah, when I swore that the waters of Noah would never again cover the earth. So now I have sworn not to be angry with you, never to rebuke you again. ¹⁰Though the mountains be shaken and the hills be removed, yet my unfailing love for you will not be shaken nor my covenant of peace be removed," says the Lord, who has compassion on you. ¹¹"Afflicted city, lashed by storms and not comforted, I will rebuild you with stones of turquoise, your foundations with lapis lazuli. ¹²I will make your battlements of rubies, your gates of sparkling jewels, and all your walls of precious stones. ¹³All your children will be taught by the Lord, and great will be their peace. ¹⁴In righteousness you will be established: Tyranny will be far from you; you will have nothing to fear. Terror will be far removed;

it will not come near you. ¹⁵If anyone does attack you, it will not be my doing; whoever attacks you will sur-render to you. ¹⁶"See, it is I who created the blacksmith who fans the coals into flame and forges a weapon fit for its work. And it is I who have created the destroyer to wreak havoc; ¹⁷no weapon forged against you will prevail, and you will refute every tongue that accuses you. This is the heritage of the servants of the Lord, and this is their vindication from me," declares the Lord. (NIV)

It took eighteen years for the purpose of Him leading me to this scripture that night to become clear. He knew I would marry young and that my husband would later abandon me. He knew I would feel like a widow, like my husband died suddenly. He knew I would feel shame and humiliation. He was right there to remind me that He is my Husband and Redeemer. Reading verse 9 here gave new meaning to rainbows for me, yet again. Not only were rainbows a sign He would never again flood the earth, but flowing into the next verse, rainbows mean more of His covenantal love, or hesed! A tangible, visible symbol that He would never stop loving me. He would never stop pursuing me. He went before me and let me know that He would be the only consistent thing in my life. He would not let me down. I know with my whole heart that God is the one and only person I can trust to never fail me. He is my everlasting covenant.

> I know with my whole heart that God is the one and only person I can trust to never fail me. He is my everlasting covenant.

I remember the week of mediation was poorly timed. Mediation fell on a Monday and I had two important eye surgeries scheduled for Tuesday and Friday of that same week. Almost poetically, Monday happened to be the anniversary of the day Chad and I met. Instead of celebrating, we spent over eight hours deliberating all of the nuances of the life we built together. I didn't have even an hour to myself to process and grieve everything that happened that day. I came straight home to my sweet babies and family who would be taking care of them the next day. Early the next morning, I was to have eye surgery. I was so thankful mediation went well, but rolling straight into surgery did not set me up for emotional success.

The Spirit was there as worship was being lifted, beckoning me to surrender my fears and helplessness.

I'm not a huge fan of needles to begin with, so getting the IV for surgery set me off. It wasn't just the pain prick of the stick, but all of the emotions from the day before. The floodgates were opened. I didn't have enough time to calm down before they wheeled me back into a twilight sedation surgery. I wasn't supposed to remember anything. Trying desperately to calm my nerves, I asked the nurses if this was the surgery I could pick what music we listened to. My doctor sweetly told me, "Well, no, that's the next one on Friday, but what do you want to listen to?" In my panic, I think I just said, "Any worship music would be amazing."

The eye surgery required the patient to be restrained (think like a warm cocoon of blankets) which I wouldn't have known if I was out of it. But because my emotions were already in overdrive, a full-fledged panic attack took over. I remember weeping as they held devices around my eye sockets so they could perform the much-needed surgery that would restore my vision. I was begging for more medicine from the anesthesiologist, but he had given me everything he could. Once the first doctor had performed his part, I was wheeled over to the doctor I knew. He had never seen me like this and warmly told me to try to just enjoy the colors as I lost my sight in my left eye. While I was mentally and emotionally terrified, something in the atmosphere was changing. I couldn't see anymore, but five out of the seven people in that room were singing "Another in the Fire", including my very own doctor!

> "There was another in the fire
> Standing next to me
> There was another in the waters
> Holding back the seas
> And should I ever need reminding
> Of how I've been set free
> There is a cross that bears the burden
> Where another died for me"

The Spirit was there as worship was being lifted, beckoning me to surrender my fears and helplessness. I was at peace enough to stop crying and watch the kaleidoscope of colors change over my eye as my doctor himself worked… and worshiped.

> "And I can see the light in the darkness
> As the darkness bows to Him"

It was perhaps the most heavenly moment I have ever experienced. The nurses and other doctors sounded like angels.

> "There is no other name

But the Name that is Jesus
He who was and still is
And will be through it all...
I know I will never be alone"

I felt my own shaky voice start to declare and sing it. I know that I will never be alone because the same one who was in the fire with those Hebrew boys back in Daniel's day was the same one there with me in the midst of my own fire.

"How good You've been to me
I'll count the joy come every battle
'Cause I know that's where You'll be"[33]

These few minutes in surgery were just a small representation of all I had been through over the last year. The fire had been refining me, doing what fire does. Burning off unholy bits, purifying, and leaving me utterly desperate for God, dependent on His sustaining power. The Refiner's fire left my heart knowing I could trust Him for everything in every aspect of my life. Not only was my physical vision restored, but my spiritual eyes had a total makeover as well.

Long before the age of podcasts, we had the radio. As children, the radio was all my siblings and I had on the thirty-minute journey into town where we went to school, church, and pretty much all other activities. From those many hours in the car my parents listened to sermons on the radio, I became well acquainted with the voice of Dr. Tony Evans. Every now and again, I'll seek out his sermons to hear that comforting, all-too-familiar voice. Something he said really stuck out to me that really hit home during this season, "A storm is always designed to increase your faith and give you a deeper experience with God. Storms aren't pleasant, they're uncomfortable and sometimes they can be life-threatening, but they always come with a purpose."[34]

This makes me think about the details of how a rainbow appears to its viewer who must be at just the right angle to see a rainbow. I won't get too scientific on you, but the person must be at a 42 degree angle looking opposite the sun.[35] In other words, the light must be behind the viewer. In order to see what God is doing with the storms in our lives, we must see our storms from the Son's perspective. We already know His goodness and mercy are chasing us down, but we must also understand Jesus has our backs so we can see things the way He does. If we let Him, He can reflect, He can refract or "break up," and He will disperse His light to show His holy view of our lives' circumstances. Only by seeing them through His perspective can we see purpose in our storm and the beauty He wants to bring from them.

In order to see what God is doing with the storms in our lives, we must see our storms from the Son's perspective.

This deeper experience of seeing things the way He does allows us to trust Him more.

When speaking on life's storms, my own pastor, JD Greear, said, "When storms hit, don't assume you're out of God's will. Certain storms are part of God's will for you, because God is not just doing something for you; he's also doing something in you."[36] I feel like a majority of the purpose in my pain was to expose the idols in my heart and to draw me closer to the heart of the Father. I may not ever fully know the entire purpose in my pain, but I do know enough right now that puts me at ease. Whatever storm I face, even if it's more suffering, I'll face it with both feet firmly planted because I trust the Lord without question. I'll never have a valid reason to doubt my Father's heart for me. My favorite hymn since I was little, "It Is Well with My Soul," has become my anthem.

> "When peace, like a river, attendeth my way,
> When sorrows like sea billows roll;
> Whatever my lot, Thou has taught me to say,
> It is well, it is well, with my soul."

Do you believe that He is good? Do you believe that He is God? Relinquish control and give Him your heavy burdens. Exchange your burdens for His peace. Let it be well with your soul. Allow the Father to be your calm in this swirling storm. He may very well let the storm continue to rage all around you, but He promises to be your peace.

> *Come to me, all you who are weary and burdened, and I will give you rest. Take my yoke upon you and learn from me, for I am gentle and humble in heart, and you will find rest for your souls. For my yoke is easy and my burden is light.* Matthew 11:28-30 (NIV)

> *The Lord's unfailing love surrounds the one who trusts in him.* Psalm 32:10 (NIV)

Y'all listen! The Lord longs to be gracious to you. He wants to be your refuge and the one you trust in. He promises us rest for our troubled souls. He promises us perfect peace and that His unfailing love will surround us if we trust in Him.

Reflection

- Have you ever doubted that God is who He says He is? Have you doubted His goodness and faithfulness?

- How can you see His hand upon your life, even in the storm?

- Ask the Father what the purpose is for the pain you've walked through. Allow Him to show you.

Everlasting Father, thank you for Your promises I can believe and rest in. Help me to trust You to show me the purpose in this awful pain. Help me to believe what You say about who I am in You. Help me to believe Your promises even when the devil is on my back tempting me to doubt Your goodness and authority in my storm. I trust You implicitly with my life, pain, purpose, and future. Have Your will in my life. Amen.

CHAPTER 10

Exploring the Everlasting Covenant

L ooking out toward the horizon, and what could be in the future, begs questions of reflection. What I know about God will help shape the way I move forward. God is faithful. He knew this heartbreak was coming, and by His loving kindness, He will continue to see me through it. He will see you through it, too. He has brought us to this place in life intentionally and for a purpose. He has given me new eyes to see life by. Be encouraged that you are not alone in your pain, your suffering, or this season you find yourself in.

I've gathered a few ideas, ten actually, that brought me peace and hope that we can exercise through this storm and any future storm that comes our way. Think of these as practical next steps that can immediately be applied and implemented.

1. Expect Big and New

The Word is full of promises of how we should be expectant. These are a couple the Lord brought to my attention repeatedly:

Look at the nations and watch— and be utterly amazed. For I am going to do something in your days that you would not believe, even if you were told. Habakkuk 1:5 (NIV)

Forget the former things; do not dwell on the past. See, I am doing a new thing! Now it springs up; do you not perceive it? I am making a way in the wilderness and streams in the wasteland. Isaiah 43:18-19 (NIV)

I will never forget the day our divorce was finalized. I thought I was good with my grief, that I had already grieved everything the day held. I was so wrong. Nothing, not even eighteen months of horrible interactions, can prepare you for that casual email from your attorney letting you know the judge granted the divorce and to have a nice weekend.

I fell to my knees. How could eighteen years of your life dedicated to another person be summed up and dismissed in two sentences? My heart was torn in two all over again. I was scheduled to attend a women's event at church that evening and between my grief and attacks from the Enemy, I did not want to go. My sweet friend pulled me up off of the bathroom floor and got me to church that evening. I was so reluctant to be there and would have preferred to just be in my bed wallowing in my grief… but God.

That night, we broke off into small groups and in His kindness and mercy, my small group was even smaller than it should've been. We had introductions and I kept mine light and short to avoid shedding more tears. But as each woman told her story, tears would still come. Hearing beautiful stories of having marriages of thirty and forty years, the sadness was too much for tears not to be shed. After the introductions were over, I will never forget what my small group leader said that night. "Don't be afraid to give up the life you always dreamed of in exchange for the life you can't even imagine." I was undone all over again. My new friend knew instantly the reason why she felt led to say that word was for me and my heart. God needed me to hear that my story was

> *"Don't be afraid to give up the life you always dreamed of in exchange for the life you can't even imagine."*

not over, that He was still working, and that I would be amazed when all was said and done!

She got up, scooped me up, and just held me while I sobbed. That night, my Savior met me in the form of this tiny blonde lady and spoke right to my heart as she gave me a fresh perspective on Ephesians 3:20. *Now to him who is able to do immeasurably more than all we ask or imagine, according to his power that is at work within us.* On a night when I wanted anything other than to be around people, the Lord used those people to be an instrument of His grace and kindness to me. More than that, I was reinvigorated with fresh hope and excitement about what the future holds for myself and my kids.

This has been a refining and sanctifying season, but it's time for something fresh and new.

He is a good Father who loves to lavish His love and surprises on His kids. Don't be too surprised when something amazing happens in the midst of your pain.

> *You were taught, with regard to your former way of life, to put off your old self, which is being corrupted by its deceitful desires; to be made new in the attitude of your minds; and to put on the new self, created to be like God in true righteousness and holiness.* Ephesians 4:22-24 (NIV)

Throughout your season of suffering, God longs to make you new. He wants to redesign the landscape of your heart and life. Isaiah prophetically challenges not to dwell on the past because the Lord is doing something new. He's reviving your spirit and making you more like Him. This has been a refining and sanctifying season, but it's time for something fresh and new.

We've probably all heard 2 Corinthians 5:17 (NLT). *This means that anyone who belongs to Christ has become a new person. The old life is*

gone; a new life has begun! For the longest time, I thought this techni-
cally only applied to a person when they first accepted Christ. As I've
walked through this fire, I've realized He *continues* to make me new.
This season has changed me, and Christ has given my heart a makeover
yet again. Similar to what Paul said in Colossians 3:10 (NIV), by His
power, I *have put on the new self, which is being renewed in knowledge
in the image of its Creator.*

2. Fix Your Eyes

> *Therefore, since we are surrounded by such a great cloud
> of witnesses, let us throw off everything that hinders and
> the sin that so easily entangles. And let us run with per-
> severance the race marked out for us, fixing our eyes on
> Jesus, the pioneer and perfecter of faith. For the joy set
> before him he endured the cross, scorning its shame, and
> sat down at the right hand of the throne of God.* Hebrews
> 12:1-2 (NIV)

> O our God, will You not judge them? For we are power-
> less against this great multitude which is coming against
> us. We do not know what to do, but our eyes are on You.
> 2 Chronicles 20:12 (AMP)

It's always tempting to get wrapped up in sin, but especially in seasons like this. You can become an easy target for the Enemy to pick off.
Self-pity is lurking around the corner. All of the worldly comforts are
easily at our disposal. Gossip? Like, how could you not? But now, more
than ever, we must aim to keep our eyes fixated on the one who paid
for it all. He paid a debt He did not owe so that we could have eternal
life, hope, and salvation. When our eyes are fixed on Him, it's so much
easier to dodge the temptations the Enemy will throw at us. When we're
locked in on His goodness and glory, the troubles of life that come our

way aren't as likely to take us down and to make us feel as if we're ruined. If we're fixated on Him, we can't help but compare our situation with what Jesus might do if faced with the same circumstances.

I'm reminded of the incredible story in Matthew 14 when the disciples are in the boat in a storm and Jesus walks on the water to join them. Peter bravely got in on the miracle and was walking on the water toward Jesus, until he looked away and saw how big the waves were. He was full of faith until he took his eyes off of Jesus and focused on the surrounding storm, then he began to sink. The implication is that if Peter had kept his eyes fixed on Jesus, he could have walked on the water all the way to Jesus. John Piper said, "Therein lies the key to the Christian life: not hard work for Jesus, not labor for Jesus, but *looking* at Jesus."[37] While laboring for the kingdom is important and necessary, it's all futile and pointless if our main focus isn't Christ.

As the old hymn "Turn Your Eyes Upon Jesus" says, when we turn our eyes upon Jesus, the things of this world will grow strangely dim in the light of His glory and grace. I think about the imagery of our trials and suffering turning black and white and all of the color is beheld in our view of the Lord. I mean, John told us in Revelation the throne He sits on is encircled by a rainbow (Rev. 4:3)! His glory overshadows everything about our earthly circumstances. Our problems don't disappear but they get more bearable when we're locked in on Him.

3. Don't Forget Who You Belong To

I knew you before I formed you in your mother's womb. Before you were born I set you apart and appointed you.
Jeremiah 1:5 (NLT)

But to all who did receive him, who believed in his name, he gave the right to become children of God.
John 1:12 (ESV)

You were once dead in your sins, but now you are alive in Christ! (Rom. 6:11) You once walked in darkness, but are now walking in the light. (Eph. 5:8) Once you felt forgotten, but now you are known and adopted by the Father! You are a child of God. You have been redeemed. You are set apart for a specific purpose. He knows every hair on your head, every thought you think, and every dream and desire of your heart. You're more than cared for, you're cherished! The Lord longs to be in constant relationship with you.

You have a Defender who will never leave you or forsake you. You have a refuge to run to. You can hide under the shadow of His wings. You are never alone. You are His workmanship and He's ordained you to do amazing things in His name.

You are His workmanship and He's ordained you to do amazing things in His name.

Remember that He goes before you and fights for you. If He is for you, who can be against you (Rom. 8:31)? Over and over throughout the Israelites' story, you see how the Lord fights for them in mighty ways.

- *Moses answered the people, "Do not be afraid. Stand firm and you will see the deliverance the Lord will bring you today. The Egyptians you see today you will never see again. The Lord will fight for you; you need only to be still." Exodus 14:13-14 (NIV)*

- *The Lord your God, who is going before you, will fight for you, as he did for you in Egypt, before your very eyes, and in the wilderness. There you saw how the Lord your God carried you, as a father carries his son, all the way you went until you reached this place. Deuteronomy 1:30-31 (NIV)*

- *You will not have to fight this battle. Take up your positions; stand firm and see the deliverance the Lord will give you, Judah and Jerusalem. Do not be afraid; do not be discouraged. Go out to face them tomorrow, and the Lord will be with you.* 2 Chronicles 20:17 (NIV)

Claim these verses as your own. He is still the same God He was way back then. Give Him your anger and need for these incredible wrongs to be righted. He is such a just Father. He will humble the proud in your life in His own, perfect timing. He will fight for you, but rest in the knowledge that the real battle is already complete and He won.

4. Remember What God's Done!

One of the biggest faith builders we can experience is to look back and remember what the Lord has done and how He has been faithful to us. Grab a journal and pour your heart out, often. *I remember the days of long ago; I meditate on all your works and consider what your hands have done* (Ps. 143:5 NIV). I promise you, when you look back, you'll see God's kindness and mercy to you in those answered prayers or even in the unanswered ones! A psalm of David's is recorded in 1 Chronicles 16 (NIV) when he said, *Give praise to the Lord, proclaim his name; make known among the nations what he has done* (vs. 8). *Remember the wonders*

> *Observing all that has transpired allows us to see how He was working everything out for our good and His glory.*

he has done, his miracles, and the judgments he pronounced (vs. 12). Our hearts are so fickle and we are so quick to forget about the amazing things God has done in our lives. Having it written down makes it easy to zoom out and admire how the Lord has moved in our situations. *Jesus replied, "You do not realize now what I am doing, but later you will understand"* (John 13:7 NIV). Journaling may allow a simple snapshot of events in the moment, but a bigger revelation later when reading back over them. Sometimes, He changes our circumstances, but other times it's our hearts that are changed. Observing all that has transpired allows us to see how He was working everything out for our good and His glory.

If journaling isn't your thing, get creative. God made you with a brilliant mind capable of so many wonderful things. My girlfriend's go-to is a vision board or a collage. It's a collection of pictures, Bible verses, and sweet things that remind her of the goodness of God. Similarly, Joshua made a monument to help the people, and the generations to come, remember (Josh. 4:20-24). I've also seen a prayer wall built over several months. Pouring your heart out to God on paper and sticking it somewhere to see how He's moved and answered that prayer or hasn't yet, but you can reflect on how He's been moving.

There are so many ways we can remember, but the point is we *must* practice remembering because the Enemy of our hearts wants us to forget the things the Father has done for us and keep us doubting. King Solomon said to write them down on the tablets of your heart in Proverbs 3. How can you do that? Do you see how remembering dares you to hope?

> *Yet I still dare to hope when I remember this: The faithful love of the Lord never ends! His mercies never cease. Great is his faithfulness; his mercies begin afresh each morning. I say to myself, "The Lord is my inheritance; therefore, I will hope in him!"* Lamentations 3:21-24 (NLT)

Refusing to forget what the Father has done in our own lives is just one way of remembering. We've been gifted the Word of God and it's packed full of stories of God's faithfulness, provision, and redemption. Dive into the Word and allow the stories to come to life. The God of the Old Testament is the same God in the New Testament. God and His people are under different covenants and sets of rules depending on the time frame, but He is the same, nonetheless. All of the old covenants point to the new covenant we are under because of the blood of Christ. I can wholeheartedly say the Old Testament has come to life more than ever during this incredibly trying season and I've been able to see more clearly how all of the various Old Testament stories point to the coming Savior.

Throughout all of Deuteronomy 8, Moses warns the Israelites against forgetting about what God has done for them as they start to believe that they can do things in their own power. Moses uses powerful language to make his point. He reminded them that God led them through the desert for forty years to humble and test them. God caused them to go hungry so that He might provide their daily bread. He warned them that their hearts would become proud and they would begin to think they were the source of their own wealth and prosperity if they forgot the Lord. Finally, if they did forget the Lord and turned to worship anything or anyone else, God would destroy them. What a picture. While we're not under this covenant anymore, the concept still applies. If we don't actively remember what God has done for us, we risk becoming proud and turning to other idols. No one or no thing is to come before our relationship

don't be surprised at the fiery trials you are going through, as if something strange were happening to you. Instead, be very glad—for these trials make you partners with Christ in his suffering, so that you will have the wonderful joy of seeing his glory when it is revealed to all the world.

with Him. If there are idols in our lives that come before Christ, we still risk being destroyed. No thanks! I'll pass. Let's remember!

5. Trade Your Grief and Allow Him to Use You so that He Might be Glorified

> *Dear friends, don't be surprised at the fiery trials you are going through, as if something strange were happening to you. Instead, be very glad—for these trials make you partners with Christ in his suffering, so that you will have the wonderful joy of seeing his glory when it is revealed to all the world.* 1 Peter 4:12-13 (NLT)

Here me out. You must grieve. It is a hard, sometimes ridiculously long journey. It is not linear, either, but eventually, there will be a bit of a clearing and you can come up for air from your grief. You'll realize it's the Lord who has been carrying you through this season.

At the risk of sounding so cliché, I want to share a specific way the Lord allowed me to trade my grief. He had me focus on and begin calling out the ways He has blessed me. Naming the little gifts from the Father allowed me to see His hand in my life. Sometimes, this looked like recognizing the individual gifts each of my children are to me and how they've been given talents. The Lord knew I would be so blessed by having a mama's boy and saw fit to fashion my littlest as such. Other times, recognizing the blessings in my life were on a much smaller scale. Blessings we take for granted so often. A bright, sunny day. Food on the table. A beautiful rainbow. Enough money to pay the bills. A perfectly timed, encouraging phone call. A friend being burdened to meet a specific need of yours. A hand-picked flower from my mama's boy. Cultivating a heart full of gratitude for all of the blessings from the Lord served me well in my grieving process. Naming

> God created you for this exact time in history. You are His masterpiece which He prepared beforehand to bring Him glory.

these blessings opened my eyes to the way the Lord works all things together, making them beautiful in His time.

Recognizing the Giver of these blessings can't help but to stir a reaction of the heart. I love these verses that are true for all believers walking by the Spirit.

> *The Spirit of the Sovereign Lord is on me, because the Lord has anointed me to proclaim good news to the poor. He has sent me to bind up the brokenhearted, to proclaim freedom for the captives and release from darkness for the prisoners, to proclaim the year of the Lord's favor and the day of vengeance of our God, to comfort all who mourn, and provide for those who grieve in Zion— to bestow on them a crown of beauty instead of ashes, the oil of joy instead of mourning, and a garment of praise instead of a spirit of despair. Isaiah 61:1-3 (NIV)*

Pray and ask yourselves some deep questions. How can God use my heartbreak? How can God get glory from my story? Am I willing to let that happen? Father, where's the beauty in this dark season of mine? How can I proclaim the good news of the gospel and the freedom that comes from it? What's next, God?

The truth is God created you for this exact time in history. You are His masterpiece which He prepared beforehand to bring Him glory. The heart behind Ephesians 2:10 is that He already created the opportunity for you do good works for the kingdom *and* He has gifted you with the power to do them! He knew you would walk through this hard season, yet He's already given you gifts and talents to accomplish your God-given purpose and bring Him glory. This past season has been a refining one, bringing out the gold in your heart and life. Your pain will not be wasted.

I found myself singing "Canvas and Clay" by Pat Barrett so loudly, declaring it over my life. I found it so comforting that nothing will be wasted and He WILL still get the glory from this!

> "I know nothing has been wasted
> No failure or mistake
> You're an artist and a potter
> I'm the canvas and the clay
> You make all things work together
> For my future and for my good
> You make all things work together
> For Your glory and for Your name
> For my good, for my good"[38]

6. Recommit to the Mission of Jesus and the Cross

> *Therefore, go and make disciples of all the nations, baptizing them in the name of the Father and the Son and the Holy Spirit. Teach these new disciples to obey all the commands I have given you. And be sure of this: I am with you always, even to the end of the age.* Matthew 28:19-20 (NLT)

Ultimately as Christians on Earth, we have one mission: to make disciples, baptize them, and teach them to obey the Lord's commands. Everything else is temporary and will fade away. Only what's done for the kingdom will matter. After my grief was mostly processed, this text brought me so much peace, hope, and inspiration going into the rest of my life.

Be courageous and let's go bring people home.

> *For God, who said, "Let light shine out of darkness," made his light shine in our hearts to give us the light of the knowledge of God's glory displayed in the face of Christ. But we*

have this treasure in jars of clay to show that this all-sur-passing power is from God and not from us. We are hard pressed on every side, but not crushed; perplexed, but not in despair; persecuted, but not abandoned; struck down, but not destroyed. We always carry around in our body the death of Jesus, so that the life of Jesus may also be revealed in our body. For we who are alive are always being given over to death for Jesus' sake, so that his life may also be revealed in our mortal body. So then, death is at work in us, but life is at work in you. It is written: "I believed; therefore I have spoken." Since we have that same spirit of faith, we also believe and therefore speak, because we know that the one who raised the Lord Jesus from the dead will also raise us with Jesus and present us with you to himself. All this is for your benefit, so that the grace that is reaching more and more people may cause thanksgiving to overflow to the glory of God. Therefore we do not lose heart. Though outwardly we are wasting away, yet inwardly we are being renewed day by day. For our light and momentary troubles are achieving for us an eternal glory that far outweighs them all. So we fix our eyes not on what is seen, but on what is unseen, since what is seen is temporary, but what is unseen is eternal. 2 Corinthians 4:6-18 (NIV)

It's so clear from this passage that the Lord wants to use our hardships to build our faith and further the kingdom. There is purpose in the pain and He won't waste it. Everything we are experiencing is fleeting. While this is extraordinary pain, we are not crushed, we are not abandoned, and we are not destroyed. But the Lord is with us and is shining His light into our dark situations. Let us open our eyes to the bigger scope of the kingdom of God. You are here at this exact time and place on purpose. How can God use your story in His bigger story that would have an eternal impact? How can we see God's power in our situation? How can we throw off everything that hinders and fix our eyes on Him? How has the Lord been stirring your heart? What is He calling you to right now? Be courageous and let's go bring people home.

7. Hold Onto Hope

Remember that He who has promised *is* faithful and He will work *all things* together for the good of those who love Him and are called according to His purpose. If it's not good yet, then He's not finished. Dare to let your heart dream again. Hold fast to hope about a better future. Choose to have an eager expectation of how God will redeem your mess. Good days are coming. They say your best days are actually ahead of you! As Christians, our real source of hope is Jesus and His coming again. That will be the best day ever. But until then, He wants us to dream again, hope for the unimaginable, and let Him exceed our expectations over and over. Once the Lord makes it clear what your purpose is in the new season, hope comes easy at first. Then reality sets in and maybe some disappointments or doubts start to make their way into your life and heart. Revisit the topic of hope again and again. Preach it to yourself. Declare it over those disappointments and doubts. He has such an amazing purpose to all of this pain if we are faithful on our end and steward it well.

I encourage you to face all of these hurts and pain of your past head on so they lose power over your heart and mind. No, you can't change what happened to you in the past, but those feelings of abandonment, rejection, betrayal, and regret don't have to define you. Be anchored to Christ and allow His promise of hope and future to wash over you. Your future is secure because of Him!

God did this so that, by two unchangeable things in which it is impossible for God to lie, we who have fled to take hold of the hope set before us may be greatly encouraged.

> *We have this hope as an anchor for the soul, firm and secure.* Hebrews 6:18-19 (NIV)

> *"For I know the plans I have for you", declares the Lord, "plans to prosper you and not to harm you, plans to give you hope and a future."* Jeremiah 29:11 (NIV)

8. Find Your Community

I'm sure you've heard someone say, "Tell me who your top five friends are, and I'll tell you who you are." Who you confide in matters. Who you do life with matters. You may be convicted to leave behind some old relationships that no longer serve your kingdom purpose or line up with your newfound identity in Christ. I challenge you to take inventory of your close relationships and dig deep. Ask yourself if they are headed in the same direction as you feel the Lord is leading you. Some may need to be pruned, but He'll faithfully supply the meaningful relationships He wants you to be in.

> *If one person falls, the other can reach out and help. But someone who falls alone is in real trouble.* Ecclesiastes 4:10 (NLT)

Surround yourself with people who love you and truly love the Lord. Resist the temptation to isolate and shut people out. *But if we are living in the light, as God is in the light, then we have fellowship with each other* (1 John 1:7 NLT). Not only is it wise to be surrounded by other believers, we're commanded to. There isn't anything quite like being reminded of the goodness and mercy of God when you're flat on your face with heartbreak. Allow them to lead you back to the feet of Jesus and carry you through the tough seasons.

Praise be to the God and Father of our Lord Jesus Christ, the Father of compassion and the God of all comfort, who comforts us in all our troubles, so that we can comfort those in any trouble with the comfort we ourselves receive from God. 2 Corinthians 1:3-4 (NIV)

Get involved with your local church if you aren't already. Scope out some small group or Bible study options and get plugged in. If there's not something readily available to participate in, you have a unique opportunity to start one. Whatever situation you find yourself in, be vulnerable to let them into your life and allow them to love on you and vice versa. This is a foundational element of discipleship.

> there is something that happens when you take on duties and other people's burdens that allow you to get out of your own head.

Another way to get involved is by serving in your local church. In a study my own church did, they found that churchgoers feel the most connected with their church when they are serving in some capacity.[39] Depending on the size of the church, I'm willing to bet there are a ton of opportunities available to slide into such as kids ministry, greeting, parking, security, and ushering just to name a few. I promise, there is something that happens when you take on duties and other people's burdens that allow you to get out of your own head. Check out Galatians 6:1-10.

9. Rest in Him

Rest is a word most Americans don't really understand or honor. In our culture, everything is hurried and hustled. There is no rest for the weary, so to speak, but it doesn't have to be like this. The Lord wants you to cast all of your burdens on Him. Everything that weighs on your heart and mind. He already knows it all; He just wants *you* to surrender it to Him. Jenny Donnelly, a guest writer for Ann Voskamp says "Rest means that we are resting in what is happening right this second with a complete trust that God will meet us in our next moment. When we are in our resting place, we aren't ignoring our responsibilities, challenges, and projects and just checking out for the sake of peace. No, Jesus calls us to sit next to Him and bring our burdens with us."[40] Allow Him to carry you and sustain you. *Even to your old age and gray hairs I am he, I am he who will sustain you. I have made you and I will carry you; I will sustain you and I will rescue you* (Isa. 46:4 NIV). He'll do it gladly and oh so lovingly, it just requires your surrender. Let Him lead you in His rhythms of grace.

> *Cast your cares on the Lord and he will sustain you; he will never let the righteous be shaken.* Psalm 55:22 (NIV)

In Matthew 6, Jesus talks about not worrying about the daily happenings like what to eat, drink, or wear. He said,

> *Look at the birds. They don't plant or harvest or store food in barns, for your heavenly Father feeds them. And aren't you far more valuable to him than they are? Can all your worries add a single moment to your life? And why worry about your clothing? Look at the lilies of the field and how they grow. They don't work or make their clothing, And if God cares so wonderfully for wildflowers that are here today and thrown into the fire tomorrow, he will certainly care for you. Why do you have so little faith?* Matthew 6:26-28,30 (NLT)

Refuse to get caught up in the what ifs and worries about the future. To be fair, the things you worry about may not ever even happen. I must confess, this passage has checked my heart and convicted me many times.

I love thinking about the flowers that pop up every year without fail. In my part of the country, daffodils, tulips, and hyacinths come up every spring. No one tells them when to start growing, except God. And every year, without fail, new life springs forth from the frozen ground that used to look dead. Not only do they smell incredible, but they're also absolutely beautiful. If He can do that with a tiny bulb, why couldn't He do it for His children He loves that much more? The fact is He goes before you and has a perfect plan.

> *Let the beloved of the Lord rest secure in him, for he shields him all day long, and the one the Lord loves rests between his shoulders.* Deuteronomy 33:12 (NIV)

10. Choose Joy and Chase Rainbows

> *I consider that our present sufferings are not worth comparing with the glory that will be revealed in us.* Romans 8:18 (NIV).

In other words, the pain that you've been feeling can't compare to the joy that's coming.

> *Weeping may last through the night, but joy comes with the morning.* Psalm 30:5 (NLT)

The song "Joy in the Morning" by Tauren Wells got popular just before our divorce was finalized. By this time, there were more days filled with joy and laughter than sorrow and crying, like at the beginning. It put words to so much of what my heart was feeling and had felt in the darkest parts

The aches and pains of this world can't compare at all to the joy that's coming.

of the journey. It filled me with unexplainable hope and excitement for what is still to come.

> "Everything happens for a reason
> But you don't know what you don't know
> And you'll never have peace if you don't let go of tomorrow
> 'Cause it ain't even faith till your plan falls apart
> But you still choose to follow, uh
> If it doesn't make sense right now, it will when it's over
> There will be joy in the morning
> There will be joy in the morning
> Giving in to your feelings is like drowning in the shadows
> Oh, you gotta keep believing
> Even in the middle of the unknown
> 'Cause grace will be there
> When you come to the end of your rope and you let go
> It may feel like you're goin' down now
> But the story isn't over
> There will be joy in the morning
> There will be joy in the morning
> If it's not good, then He's not done
> No, He's not done with it yet
> There will be joy in the morning"[41]

Between John 14 and 16, Jesus prepared His disciples for His inevitable death and promised them the Holy Spirit once He left them behind. Jesus acknowledged that they would be sad, but repeated the idea that their grief would turn to joy. He compared this to a woman going through the pain of labor and delivery, but soon forgetting her pain once she holds her new baby. She's then overcome with joy. The aches and pains of this world can't compare at all to the joy that's coming. Ultimately, this is not our home and we have the hope of heaven and life eternal with the Lord to look forward to. When we get there, the troubles of this world will be long forgotten; however, we can still have this joy while we're here, right in the middle of our mess. I've learned that joy is not an elusive feeling; it's the awareness of my need for grace and finding that in Christ. It is a conscious choice to choose joy in the midst of sadness. The joy of the Lord is your strength.

Chin up, friend. Your story isn't over. You are chosen and redeemed. Allow the Lord to change your perspective. See the beautiful rainbow He is shining over you and your storm. There is still beauty in this crazy life. Every day there are breathtaking sunrises and sunsets… and rainbows. Behold His glory.

> *Like the appearance of a rainbow in the clouds on a rainy day, so was the radiance around him. This was the appearance of the likeness of the glory of the Lord.* Ezekiel 1:28 (NIV)

The Lord is still on the throne radiating glory, encircled by a rainbow, and writing redemption stories every day! Saturate yourself in His promises. Claim them over your life so, in turn, you reflect the light of Jesus to those around you. Let His everlasting covenant hold you fast. Rest assured that if it's not good, then He's not done yet.

Reflection

- Of these ten steps, which are your top three you're feeling convicted to take action on?

- How do you think the Lord could change your heart and life by taking even one of these steps?

- For the sake of accountability, who can you tell about these steps you feel led to take and ask them to hold you to taking action? What kind of time frame can you aim for to see movement in these areas?

Almighty Father, we praise You! You are sovereign. You are good and reign over all! Thank you for giving us hope and a future to look forward to. We are Yours and surrender our story to You. We know that while we still may be in the midst of a mess, You are not done writing our story. You will get the glory. Help us to keep our eyes fixed on You and recognize all of the good things in our life are gifts from You. Let us be satisfied with Your love. Let us know that our peace, joy, and hope are found in Your love. May Your promises ever be before us and may the joy we get from knowing You be our strength until we see You in glory. Thank you, Lord, for giving us fresh eyes to see life with. Amen.

About the Author

Rachel Leigh is the author of Chasing Rainbows: A Journey from Broken Promises to the Everlasting Covenant. She wrote it to serve as faith-filled encouragement to anyone walking through their own season of suffering and waiting. Having graduated with her bachelor's in communications from Trevecca Nazarene University, her faith and identity in Christ have been of first importance. As a former licensed banker, her passion was helping her clients succeed financially, which has now evolved into encouraging others to find their identity in Christ, seeing themselves as the Father sees them. Rachel loves singing worship music, spending time with friends and family, traveling, and gardening. She aims to visit all the U.S. National Parks in her lifetime. She lives in Raleigh, North Carolina with her three children.

Endnotes

Preface

[1] Elliot, Elisabeth, Suffering Is Never for Nothing, B&H Publishing Group, 2019.

Chapter 1–Broken Promises

[2] Elevation Worship and Maverick City Music featuring Chandler Moore and Naomi Raine, "Jireh," Chris Brown/Steven Furtick/Chandler Moore/Naomi Raine, released 04/30/2021. Essential Music Publishing and Bethel Music Publishing, 2 Old Church Basement, 2021, Spotify.

[3] Elevation Worship and Maverick City Music featuring Chandler Moore and Naomi Raine, "Jireh," Chris Brown/Steven Furtick/Chandler Moore/Naomi Raine, released 04/30/2021. Essential Music Publishing and Bethel Music Publishing, 2 Old Church Basement, 2021, Spotify.

[4] Hillsong UNITED, "Whole Heart (Hold Me Now)–Live" Joel Houston/Aodhan King, released 04/26/2019, Capitol CMG Publishing, 4 People (Live), 2019, Spotify.

Chapter 2–Unwanted Weeds of the Heart

[5] Made for This hosted by Jennie Allen, Fourteenth episode "Forgiveness is a Decision AND a Process with

Lysa Terkeurst," https://podcasts.apple.com/ca/podcast/
made-for-this-with-jennie-allen/id1466667116?i=1000498300730

Chapter 3–Storms Don't Last Forever

6   Avital Snow, "The Meaning of Hesed: Hebrew for Love,"
    published May 27, 2021, https://firmisrael.org/learn/
    the-meaning-of-hesed-hebrew-for-love/

7   "Chesed," Wikipedia, last modified July14, 2023, https://en.wiki-
    pedia.org/wiki/Chesed

8   CeCe Winans, "Believe for It," Mitch Wong/Dwan Hill/Kyle Lee/
    CeCe Winans, released 03/12/2021, Integrity Music/Fun Attic
    Music/Endurance Music Group/Pure Psalms Music, 15 Believe
    For It, 2021, Spotify.

Chapter 4–A Sunset With the Gardener

9   Elisabeth Elliot, A Path Through Suffering, Revell a division of
    Baker Publishing Group, 2003

10 Dave Furman, "If God loves you, He will prune you," The Gospel
    Coalition, February 28, 2018, https://www.thegospelcoalition.org/
    article/god-prunes-those-he-loves/

11 Lysa TerKeurst, It's Not Supposed to be This Way, Thomas
    Nelson, 2018.

Chapter 5–The Already and the Not Yet

12 Dr. David Jeremiah. "Joseph: Overcoming Disappointments."
    February 19, 2019. Location Unknown YouTube. Running time 1
    hour 2 minutes https://www.youtube.com/watch?v=4S5E2CRjSkk

13 A.W. Tozer, The Root of the Righteous, Moody Publishers, 2015.

14 Christa Smith. "Letting God Finish Your Story." February 5,
    2019. Expression58 Church Los Angeles, California. YouTube.

Running time 1 hour 2 minutes https:// www.youtube.com/ watch?v=KiPBM_EMGg4

15   Bill Johnson. "The Power of Choosing Joy." August 21, 2022. Bethel Church, Redding California. YouTube. Running Time 41 minutes. https://www.youtube.com/watch?v=u22XtGOHbRw

16   Mei Au, "God's Great Mercy in Judgment," First 5, read September 20, 2022, Mobile Application.

17   JD Greear, "The Blank Spaces." August 28, 2022. Summit Church Raleigh, North Carolina, live. Running time 46 minutes. https:// summitchurch.com/message/the-blank-spaces

18   Kellye Schiffner Carver, "Don't Judge a Book by Its Title," First 5, read August 29, 2002, Mobile Application.

19   JD Greear, Daily Devotional, "The Resurrection Shows God Is Always Moving," February 7, 2022

20   Kari Jobe, "Your Nature–Live," Jacob Sooter/Kari Jobe Carnes/ Hank Bentley/Charles Starling, released 10/23/2020, Capitol CGM Publishing and Essential Music Publishing LLC, 10 The Blessing (Live), 2020, Spotify.

21   JD Greear, "Surely Goodness and Mercy Will Follow Me," May 15, 2022, Summit Church Raleigh, North Carolina, live. Running time 51 minutes. https://summitchurch.com/message/ surely-goodness-and-mercy-will-follow-me

Chapter 6–My "Yes" is on the Table

22   Bill Johnson. "Our Divine Purpose." December 4, 2022. Bethel Church, Redding California. YouTube. Running Time 49 minutes. https://www.youtube.com/watch?v=c0TcMuhKtXM

23   Cody Carnes, "Firm Foundation (He Won't)," Cody Carnes/ Austin Davis/Chandler Moore, released 01/03/2022, Capitol CGM Publishing and Essential Music Publishing, 1 Firm Foundation (He Won't), 2022, Spotify.

Chapter 7–I Will Not Be Silent

[24] Hillsong UNITED, "Whole Heart (Hold Me Now)–Live" Joel Houston/Aodhan King, released 04/26/2019 Capitol CMG Publishing, 4 People (Live), 2019, Spotify.

[25] Steven Furtick. "Kept In The Dark." December 5, 2021. Elevation Church, Charlotte, North Carolina. YouTube. Running time 1 hour 7 minutes. https://www.youtube.com/watch?v=rED5LDxajuc&t=2s

[26] Bill Johnson. "The War in Your Head." April 2, 2022. Bethel Church, Redding California. YouTube. Running Time 43 minutes. https://www.youtube.com/watch?v=OWXxVSDqI4U

[27] Susie Larson, Strong in Battle: Why the Humble Will Prevail, Bethany House Publishers, 2022.

Chapter 8–Does Jesus Really Know How I Feel?

[28] Elliot, Elisabeth, Suffering Is Never for Nothing, B&H Publishing Group, 2019.

[29] Bethel Worship, "Son of Suffering–Live," Matt Redman/Aaron Moses/David Funk/Nate Moore, released 09/24/2021, Essential Music Publishing LLC/Integrity Music/Bethel Music Publishing, 4 Homecoming (Live), 2021, Spotify.

Chapter 9–The Arms That Hold Me Now

[30] Phillip Keller, A Shepherd Looks at Psalm 23, Zondervan, 2007

[31] JD Greear. "I Have No Needs." May 1, 2022. Summit Church Raleigh, North Carolina, live. Running time 41 minutes. https://summitchurch.com/message/i-have-no-needs

[32] Elliot, Elisabeth, Suffering Is Never for Nothing, B&H Publishing Group, 2019.

[33] Hillsong UNITED, "Another In The Fire–Live," Joel Houston/Chris Davenport, released 04/26/2019, Capitol CMG Publishing, 10 People (Live), 2019, Spotify.

[34]   Dr. Tony Evans. "Trusting God in a Storm." January 5, 2020. Oak Cliff Bible Fellowship, Dallas, Texas. YouTube. Running time 28 minutes. https://www.youtube.com/watch?v=hw40v_QM6Bw

[35]   "Rainbow," National Geographic, accessed April 25, 2023, https://education.nationalgeographic.org/resource/rainbow/

[36]   JD Greear, Daily Devotional, "You Can't Go Over or Around The Storm," Dec 27, 2022.

Chapter 10–Exploring the Everlasting Covenant

[37]   John Piper, "How to Keep Your Eyes on Christ," Desiring God, Episode 1895, February 1, 2023. https://www.desiringgod.org/interviews/how-to-keep-your-eyes-on-christ

[38]   Pat Barrett, "Canvas and Clay," Ben Smith/Christ Tomlin/Pat Barrett, released 09/25/2019, Capitol CMG Publishing, 17 Act Justly, Love Mercy, Walk Humbly, 2021, Spotify

[39]   "The Summit Church Annual Survey," The Summit Church, poll completed 2017.

[40]   Jenny Donnelly, "The Search For Rest In A Hurry-Up World," Ann Voskamp, January 2020, https://annvoskamp.com/2020/01/the-search-for-rest-in-a-hurry-up-world/

[41]   Tauren Wells, "Joy in the Morning," Chris Brown/Steven Furtick/Tauren Wells released 06/10/2022, Essential Music Publishing LLC. 8 Joy In The Morning, 2022, Spotify.

Printed in the USA
CPSIA information can be obtained
at www.ICGtesting.com
JSHW011221271123
52528JS00012B/369